FOUR CORNERS

THE VINEYARDS AND WINERIES OF NEW MEXICO, ARIZONA, UTAH AND COLORADO

BY

STARLEY TALBOTT

Printed in the United States of America

International Standard Book Number
978-0-9762943-1-3

Published by
Plainstar Press
1555 Main Street, Suite A3-180
Windsor, CO 80550
www.starleytalbott.com

TABLE OF CONTENTS

INTRODUCTION v

NEW MEXICO 1

VIVAC WINERY 3

BLACK MESA WINERY 7

JACONA VALLEY VINEYARD 11

PONDEROSA VALLEY WINERY 15

ANASAZI FIELDS WINERY 23

CASA RONDEÑA WINERY 29

TIERRA ENCANTADA VINEYARDS AND WINERY 33

TULAROSA VINEYARDS 37

HEART OF THE DESERT VINEYARDS 43

LA VIÑA WINERY 47

SOUTHWEST WINES 51

ARIZONA 55

COLIBRI VINEYARD AND WINERY 57

CHARRON VINEYARDS 63

CALLAGHAN VINEYARDS 65

CANELO HILLS VINEYARD AND WINERY 69

SONOITA VINEYARDS 75

ALCANTARA VINEYARDS 79

JEROME WINERY 83

PAGE SPRINGS VINEYARDS AND CELLARS 89

UTAH 95

SPANISH VALLEY VINEYARDS AND WINERY 97

CASTLE CREEK WINERY 101

COLORADO 105

    TWO RIVERS WINERY AND CHATEAU 107

    GRANDE RIVER VINEYARDS 113

    COLORADO CELLARS 119

    CARLSON VINEYARDS 123

    REEDER MESA VINEYARDS 129

    LEROUX CREEK INN AND VINEYARDS 133

    STONE COTTAGE CELLARS 137

    TERROR CREEK VINEYARD AND WINERY 141

    CIATANO WINERY 145

    AUGUSTINA'S WINERY 149

    BALISTRERI VINEYARDS 153

    SPRUCE MOUNTAIN MEADERY 157

    THE WINERY AT HOLY CROSS ABBEY 161

    GUY DREW VINEYARDS 165

APPENDIX 169

SELECTED BIBLIOGRAPHY 180

ACKNOWLEDGEMENTS 181

ABOUT THE AUTHOR 182

INTRODUCTION

Under all is the land; upon its wise use depend the survival and growth of our civilization—from the preamble to the Realtors Code of Ethics.

All cultures depend on the land and use it for sustenance. For thousands of years, the land that now comprises the four corner states of the United States—Arizona, Colorado, New Mexico, and Utah—was grazing land for herds of bison, elk, deer and antelope. It also sustained the ancient peoples who lived as hunter-gatherers, and as farmers, in some areas.

The first Europeans settled in North America in the 1500's, when Spanish explorers traveled from New Spain (Mexico) to the territories that later became the states of New Mexico, Arizona, Utah, Colorado, California, and Texas. They established farms and ranches and introduced animals and crops that were new to the area. Over time, agricultural practices changed and evolved, and different crops replaced others. Modern farmers are attempting to follow methods that conserve the land and water, from which all cultures thrive. A crop that has received renewed attention is the grapevine.

New Mexico is said to be the oldest grape growing region in the United States. Spanish missionaries planted vineyards with Mission grapes and made wine, to fill their need for sacramental wine. In 1598, Don Juan de Oñate led a small band of Spanish colonists from New Spain northward, up the trail that became known as El Camino Real, the Royal Road. These colonists settled the fertile valley of the Rio Grande, in what is now New Mexico, where they established their farms.

Franciscan monks accompanied the settlers, to minister to their spiritual needs and bring the Holy Faith to the Indians. These monks celebrated mass every day, where it was necessary to serve wine, representing the Blood of Christ. The wine had to be shipped from Spain, to Mexico, and then carted a thousand miles by ox-cart to the new settlements. Spanish government officials, concerned about protecting revenues from the wine trade with the colonists, prohibited the raising of grapes and making wine in the New World. This ban was in effect for more than 150 years, however, in the remote regions of the Spanish Empire, including New Mexico and Arizona, the church chose to ignore the ban.

The first grapevines planted in what is now New Mexico were brought in 1629 to Senecu, an Indian pueblo, south of the present day town of Socorro. The cuttings that were brought by the missionaries were a variety of *Vitis vinifera*, commonly called the Mission grape. Historians think it is a European variety from Spain, called *Monica*.

Vineyards and wineries grew and continued to prosper in New Mexico until the late 1800's. By the early 1900's, the weather, including frequent floods on the Rio Grande, and the proliferation of California wineries, contributed to the decline of New Mexico's wine industry. When prohibition was enacted in 1919, making the production of wine illegal, most wineries ceased production; although, a few vineyards and wineries continued to operate despite the ban. By the time Prohibition was repealed in 1934, these wineries found they could not compete with wine from California. Then, in 1943, the greatest Rio Grande floods of the century destroyed vineyards throughout New Mexico's wine country, basically ending the wine business.

Wine production did not revive in New Mexico until 1977, when New Mexico's oldest contemporary winery, La Viña, was founded. In the 1980's European investors, attracted by low-cost land, planted thousands of grapes in southern New Mexico. Many of these vineyards failed, due to weather, disease, and marketing problems. However, by 1990 other vineyards were planted, and wineries opened throughout New Mexico. Wine festivals were established to aid in marketing, and the new wine industry in New Mexico began to blossom. New Mexico has three areas that have been designated as appellations—Mesilla Valley, Middle Rio Grande Valley, and Mimbres Valley. An appellation is a wine-growing region with officially recognized boundaries. Appellation designations are required on wine labels to identify the origin of the grapes used in making the wine. In North America there are three classes of appellations: states/provinces and counties, as well as regions more specifically defined by actual growing conditions, known as American Viticultural Areas (AVAs). However, New Mexico has divided the state into designated wine trails for tourism purposes—these are the Northern Wine Trail, Central Wine Trail, Southeast Wine Trail, and Southern Wine Trail.

Spanish explorers had also ventured into Arizona in the 1500's, and by the late 1600's, the Jesuit priest, Padre Eusebio Francisco Kino, established missions in Arizona. Padre Kino, known as a humanitarian, farmer, cattle rancher, and explorer, traveled through southern Arizona spreading the Catholic faith and teaching people how to farm. These farmers raised grapes and made wine for the church and their own use.

Arizona's modern day wine industry began in 1973, when Dr. Gordon Dutt and A. Blake Brophy established an experimental vineyard near Sonoita. Dr. Dutt, a retired soil scientist, discovered grapes flourished in the sun-baked climate of Arizona. Other vineyards soon sprouted in southeastern Arizona, followed by wine production. And, by the 1990's, there were several vineyards and wineries in central Arizona. Arizona has one American Viticultural Area in the Sonoita area.

Colorado's European settlers grew grapes and produced wine, beginning in the 1860's. Most of these early wines were made for home consumption from Concord grapes, grown on farms or in home gardens.

Vineyards in Colorado, at the present time, are located mostly on the western slope of Colorado. However, no grapes were grown there in the 1860's and 1870's, because a treaty with the Ute Indians gave them ownership of the land west of the Continental Divide in Colorado, "forever." Gold miners were the first to break the treaty, however, and settlers soon found the area held excellent agricultural prospects. The Ute Indians were moved to Utah in 1881, and people scrambled into the warm valleys of western Colorado to establish farms and ranches. These settlers brought fruit and grapevine stocks into what became known as the Grand Valley.

This area became a favorable location for growing all types of fruit, because the surrounding mesas retain the heat of the day and reflect it into the valley below, thus providing for longer frost-free seasons. Canyon winds also waft over the crops to lessen the effects of late spring or early autumn frosts. There is also ample water for irrigation from the Colorado River.

Grapes were grown and some wine produced, but the state of Colorado adopted prohibition even before the United States made the production of wine illegal in 1919. Most of the vineyards on the western slope were uprooted and re-planted with peach orchards. These orchards flourished, and the Grand Valley became known for producing some of the finest peaches in America.

When a bad freeze in the winter of 1962-63 destroyed many of the peach trees in the Grand Valley, it was thought wine grapes might be a good alternative crop, because they bud later than fruit trees. Some farmers in western Colorado were willing to try planting commercial vineyards, and a new wine industry became a reality several years later.

In the 1970's, the United States government, through the "Four Corners Regional Commission" established a research project to examine alternative sources of income for farmers in the Southwest. The agency gave a grant to Colorado State University, which was to be used for the exploration of wine grape cultivation. They established research centers in several Colorado and Utah locations.

Dr. Gerald Invancie and Jim Seewald, hobby winemakers, are recognized as the founders of Colorado's modern wine industry. Gerald Invancie and his wife, Mary, opened the first commercial winery in Denver, Colorado in 1969, making wine from California grapes.

Jim Seewald and a group of investors created Colorado Mountain Vineyards, near Palisade, Colorado, in 1980. Jim and Ann Seewald were responsible for establishing Colorado's first American Viticultural Area in the Grand Valley. Colorado Mountain Vineyards was later sold and the name changed to Colorado Cellars, which is now the oldest winery in Colorado.

Colorado's second American Viticultural Area was established in the West Elk Mountain area in 2001. The name comes from the West Elk Mountain Range that overlooks the high altitude growing area of the North Fork Valley of the Gunnison River.

A few vineyards were also established in Colorado's southwest corner, near the area where the four states form a common border, known as Four Corners. Some grapes are still grown on the eastern

STARLEY TALBOTT

side of the Continental Divide; but many of the facilities there make wine from Colorado's western slope grapes.

The first wine grapes were planted in Utah in the 1860's, soon after the initial settlement of the area by the Mormons. Restrictive liquor laws, observed by the Mormons, soon led to the abandonment of most of the vineyards. However, a young vintner named John C. Naegle operated a Wine Mission in Toquerville with the blessing of Mormon Church officials. Naegle built a big rock house with a wine cellar underneath, large enough to accommodate a wagon and a team of horses. He installed vats, presses, and other equipment, storing the wine in 500-gallon casks. By the late 1880's, however, Naegle was forced to move his business to Mexico, ending the wine industry in Utah. Naegle's home and wine cellar later became a national historic landmark. A century later, in the late 1980's, Utah's wine renaissance began when vineyards were planted in the eastern part of the state. Utah's liquor laws have been relaxed somewhat, but are still formidable obstacles to the growth of the wine industry. There are a few hardy modern day pioneers struggling to produce excellent Utah wines and make them known throughout the United States.

The long history of wine is interwoven with the culture of mankind. No one knows for sure who grew the first grapes or produced the first wine, but wine is thought to have originated in the Mediterranean area thousands of years ago. Because of its concentrated sugars and ample juice, wine may have been one of the first things man created by accident, since the grape is one fruit that has a tendency to ferment on its own.

Over the course of thousands of years, the process of winemaking was refined. Wine has played an important role in religion and social exchange since ancient times; it is sometimes used as a medicinal substance; it is an important beverage used to accompany and enhance food; and it has been the subject of much recent research and controversy as to its health benefits.

The land comprising the Four Corners states of the United States—a unique area where the boundaries of the states of Arizona, Colorado, New Mexico and Utah, touch in one location—is a prime new wine production area for visitors to explore.

This book begins the exploration in the state of New Mexico, where the oldest grapevines grew in the United States. Visitors can begin the trail in northern New Mexico, travel through central and southern New Mexico; cross into Arizona's southeastern corner; travel to central Arizona; cross briefly into Colorado's southwest corner; and then to Utah's wine country on the state's eastern border; from there it's a short drive to the Grand Valley and West Elk Mountains on Colorado's western slope; travel over the Continental Divide to the front range of the Rocky Mountains; moving down the I-25 corridor, and ending in southern Colorado.

The intention is to include all currently operating wineries—with a listing of name, location, and other information. Those selected for feature stories were based on the attributes of location, small and large, old and new, traditional and unique operations, and the ability to host visitors. Readers are invited to discover the fascinating culture of wine that is still evolving over time. Take an armchair or real journey—follow the grapevine trails of the four corners states—exploring new wine trails in the Old West. ☙

NEW MEXICO

VIVAC WINERY IN NORTHERN NEW MEXICO.

CHRIS AND JESSE PADBERG POSE WITH THEIR DOG, OSITA, (LITTLE BEAR) AT THEIR VINEYARD NEAR DIXON, NEW MEXICO.

VIVAC WINERY

Dixon, New Mexico

From the dust of the desert landscape, set amongst ragged vermilion rock spires and oceans of sea green brush, Chris and Jesse Padberg built an outpost called Vivac Winery. The name Vivac is derived from *bivouac*, a term meaning the last place to obtain food or drink before heading into the mountains.

The tiny rust-colored adobe building, on highway 68, between Taos and Santa Fe, New Mexico, is no longer the last place you can buy provisions. But, it is certainly one of the most unique attractions along the road.

The Padberg brothers were born and raised in Dixon, New Mexico. Chris attended the University of Tulane in New Orleans for three years before transferring to and graduating from the University of New Mexico, in 2001, with a history degree. Jesse earned his college degree in Spanish Literature from the University of Colorado at Boulder.

Inspired by the lifestyle of people throughout France and Italy, the Padberg brothers embarked on their mission in 1998—to make the best wine possible and have a good time doing it. They worked at construction jobs for five years so they could pursue their dream of building a winery. They began reading every publication they could find about grapes and winemaking and completed extension winemaking classes from the University of California, Davis.

"At every turn, as we began our journey to become winemakers, people were there to help us out," Chris said. Every spare penny and every spare hour was spent pursuing their dream, and, finally, on November 1, 2003, Vivac Winery opened its doors. It was deemed a great success by the Padberg brothers and continues to "grow each year."

A few miles away from the tasting room, just outside the tiny village of Dixon, is the Padberg farm, where the vineyard and wine production facility is located. "We feel that so many wines are not all that they can be," Jesse said. "We try to make every decision in the cellar count towards making a better wine."

The brothers began in the vineyard by using management practices that are mostly organic in nature. They grow the grape

SOME OF THE WINES AVAILABLE AT VIVAC WINERY.

varieties of Baca Noir, Leon Millot, and Marechal Foch, all French
hybrid varieties, suited to their cool climate at a high altitude of 6,000
feet. They use sheep and goat manure for fertilizer. They also fertilize
by using pommace (leftover stems, seeds and skins of harvested
grapes) that is aged for one year and then spread on the vineyard.
They use a minimal amount of chemicals and plan to become
certified as organic in the future. They also install bird netting before
harvest to keep the birds from eating too many grapes.

The two-acre vineyard site is known as the "fire vineyard," and
there is a story behind the name. It seems the Padberg brothers, at
the ages of six and seven, loved to shoot off fireworks at the family's
annual Fourth of July celebration. "One of our rockets landed in a field
of grass that caught on fire. The fire department had to come and put
it out. That field was known thereafter as the fire field, and after the
vineyard was planted, it became the fire vineyard," Chris said.

After the grapes are harvested, the wines are aged in both
stainless steel tanks and oak barrels. "We always age our wines in
French oak barrels, because we feel they are the best," Jesse said.
"We don't fine or filter our wines to ensure maximum flavor intensity.
And, after bottling, we won't release a wine until it has sat for at least
two months and come back together as a wine," he added.

The brothers say they learn something new about winemaking every day. They credit a great deal of their success to their families and other winemakers. "We all try to help each other out," Chris said. Chris is married to Liliana Zavala and they have a son, Maddox Zavala Padberg. Jesse is married to Michele Alexandra Bartley, and they have a son, Denim Diesel Padberg. Both Liliana and Michele have studied to be sommeliers (wine stewards) and help out at the winery. Michele is an artist, painting in bright colors in the style of "intuitive painting."

Another artist, Randall LaGro, designs the labels for Vivac Winery. LaGro is originally from New York and was trained at the Academy of Art in San Francisco. He now specializes in printmaking and monotypes; it is said that his images are "laden with the poetic and the beautiful, the fierce and the brutal, unique peeks into the subconscious."

The labels LaGro created for Vivac Winery reflect the Spanish-inspired names chosen by the Padberg brothers. Featured wines include **Divino**, from the Heaven and Hell wine series, a complex wine with bright acidity and flavors of raspberries, dark chocolate and lilacs. The **Diavolo** wine is from the Heaven and Hell series, a full-bodied and intense wine with flavors of dark berry, mint, butterscotch and vanilla. **Dolcetto** is a medium-bodied wine with flavors of dark berry, lush and smoky. The grapes for the **Fire Vineyard Estate Wine**, a wine with flavors of ripe, robust, dark fruit are grown at the Dixon Fire Vineyard.

The Padberg brothers purchase some of the grapes for their wines from other growers, but all are 100 percent New Mexico-grown grapes. And, unlike most wineries, the Padbergs do not produce any sweet wines.

In the future, the brothers intend to plant several more acres of their own vineyards, with the hope of having approximately 5,000 vines. As Chris and Jesse roam their vineyard, their furry, white dog, Osita, often accompanies them. She has a Spanish name, too, meaning "Little Bear."

Each autumn a festival called "The Dixon Studio Tour" enhances the festive nature of the countryside near Vivac Winery. More than forty local artists display their work during the two-day event.

At Vivac Winery guests can indulge in "fine wine, fine art and handmade chocolates." When in northern New Mexico, the Padberg brothers invite visitors to join them at "your high altitude refuge." ✳

THE ARTISTRY OF LYNDA BURD IS DISPLAYED ON AN
ADOBE FENCE NEAR BLACK MESA WINERY.

THE TASTING ROOM AT BLACK MESA WINERY.

BLACK MESA WINERY
Velarde, New Mexico

Charcoal cliffs, cobalt river, calico cats, and crimson wine—form the essence of Black Mesa Winery, in the Española Valley, of northern New Mexico. Soaring volcanic cliffs, with the majestic Rio Grande flowing nearby, flank the vineyard and winery. Located 45 minutes south of Taos, and 45 minutes north of Santa Fe, the winery is mid-way between those historic towns.

Established in 1992, Black Mesa Winery was sold to Jerry and Lynda Burd in 2000. The former owners, Gary and Connie Anderson, stayed for a year to help the Burds get established. "We couldn't have been successful without their help," Jerry said.

The Burds had previously lived in California and Oregon. They loved the colors of New Mexico—Lynda is an artist and Jerry wanted to remove himself from an indoor job—to work that required being outside. Jerry had received some winemaker training in Oregon, so the move to Black Mesa Winery seemed like a perfect fit for the couple.

After purchasing the business, the Burds set about stamping their artistic mark on New Mexico. Lynda painted traditional southwestern icons on the adobe fence surrounding their home, next to the vineyards and winery. She also designed cards, posters, and labels for Black Mesa Winery.

Jerry worked to maintain the vines, including Merlot, Chardonnay, Cabernet Franc, Pinot Gri, Muscat, Syrah, Riesling and Monte Pul Ciano. He also became acquainted with the microclimate of the Española Valley and its other vintners.

"A late spring frost is the biggest problem most grape growers in northern New Mexico face," Jerry said. "We are quite fortunate in our valley, in that a frost will often bounce right over the top of us. Fruit orchards of apples, peaches and cherries grow well in this area, so it follows that grapes will also do well here," he added.

"Every vineyard is different, so the most important thing I've learned is to find out what grows here and work with that information. It's also been wonderful to have the cooperation and help of other

JERRY BURD TALKS ABOUT THE MATURITY OF THE
RIPENING GRAPES AT HIS BLACK MESA WINERY.

winemakers in the area. We all kind of look out for each other and
offer what we've learned to others," Jerry said.

"My greatest mentor, and someone I learn the lesson of the day
from, is Henry Street of Ponderosa Valley Vineyards and Winery,"
Jerry emphasized. Henry Street, in addition to being a mentor
for vintners, is a historian. He has written and self-published a
booklet titled, "The History of Wine in New Mexico—400 Years of
Struggle."

Street said Franciscan monks came to New Mexico in 1598,
planted grapes and made wine for sacramental use, despite a ban on
that endeavor by Spain. Others entered the wine business and by 1800
New Mexico was considered to be "wine country," with the industry
surviving ups and downs for more than a century. However, in 1919,
Prohibition halted commercial production of wine throughout the
United States. When Prohibition ended, growers faced competition
from California, and the mighty Rio Grande River finally halted
production, with a 1943 flood of the century, destroying vineyards
throughout the state.

It was not until the 1980's that new vineyards were planted. Cold-hardy French hybrid grapes were planted in northern New Mexico. An upsurge in plantings was seen in the next ten years throughout the state. But, the new growers had failed to develop a market for the wine. Once again, many acres of grapes were abandoned.

By 1990, the newly flourishing wine business in New Mexico began to regroup itself by organizing several statewide wine festivals. These proved to be quite successful and a solid market has slowly developed.

Jerry Burd is one of the new vintners helping to establish that market. "I've seen major strides in the last five years in promoting New Mexico wines. It's important for us all to work together. I feel I need to give back to the industry and share what I've learned," he said. He also encourages visitors to explore the nearby historic districts in and around the towns of Santa Fe and Taos.

The town of Taos holds dozens of artist galleries and is famed for its Native American history. It also holds hundreds of years of Spanish influence including a grand central plaza. Just north of the town is the World Heritage Site of the Old Village of Taos Pueblo where Native Americans have resided for centuries.

Santa Fe is the capital of New Mexico and the oldest capital city in North America. It was settled in 1609 by a Spanish conquistador and became the seat of power for the Spanish Empire in its territory north of the Rio Grande. Santa Fe is the site of both the oldest public building in America, the Palace of the Governors, and the nation's oldest community celebration, the Santa Fe Fiesta, established in 1712. Santa Fe also includes many artist galleries and an open-air market on the central plaza.

After visiting in either Taos or Santa Fe it's an easy drive to Black Mesa Winery, located at mile marker 15, Highway 68, near the village of Velarde.

When guests arrive at Black Mesa Winery, they'll often see one of the many winery cats, roaming the vineyard and grounds. "The cats chase away the birds that love to eat those luscious, ripe grapes," Jerry said. Even though the cats do their best, Jerry still has to put netting over the vines to keep the birds from eating too many grapes before harvest.

HARRIETT ABBOTT PICKS MERLOT GRAPES THAT
WILL BE SOLD TO BLACK MESA WINERY.

Black Mesa Winery produces about 5,000 cases of wine each year, in several varieties, ranging from a dry white wine to a sweet red wine. Jerry has found he prefers to ferment his wines in both polyvinyl and stainless steel tanks. He ages all of his red wines in either American or French oak. He also purchases grapes from other growers in New Mexico.

The signature wines at Black Mesa Winery are **Coyote**— a blend of Cabernet Sauvignon, Petite Sirah and Zinfandel; and **Black Beauty**—a sweet red wine with a chocolate flavor. Black Mesa wines have won numerous awards in international competition.

Another wine that is causing quite a sensation is **Desenzano, 2006**. It is a blend of Tempranillo, Refosco and Carignane grapes. The wines were individually fermented and placed in oak barrels for more than a year. Then they were blended together and placed back into a combination of French and American oak for almost 6 months before bottling.

By far, though, **Black Beauty** is the favorite wine produced by Black Mesa Winery. The owners say of **Black Beauty**, "a little chocolate, a little sweetness, a little naughty, it could lead to dancing." ✤

Jacona Valley Vineyard
Santa Fe, New Mexico

Like spring bud break on a grapevine, history is bursting from the sandy soil at Jacona Valley Vineyard, 20 miles north of the historic city of Santa Fe, New Mexico. The "mother vine," at the front entrance of a house, which once served as a supply store for travelers, is said to have arrived in Santa Fe in the 1800's with Bishop Lamy.

The old mercantile building, where the vine now grows, was situated on the main road leading to Los Alamos. During the Manhattan project, a secret project for the development of the atomic bomb in the early 1940's, the scientists and their families often stopped to buy provisions on their way to and from Los Alamos. The building served as the home of several previous owners. It was also the original home for Trey and Blair Naylor, who moved there in 1998.

THIS GRAPEVINE, BROUGHT TO NEW MEXICO BY A CATHOLIC BISHOP, IS HUNDREDS OF YEARS OLD AND CALLED THE "MOTHER VINE".

TREY NAYLOR TAKES A SAMPLE OF WINE FROM A BARREL FOR A WINE TASTING AT HIS JACONA VALLEY VINEYARD AND WINERY.

The "mother vine" forms an archway in front of the "old house," its thick, green leaves and heavy main stalk are a testament to its hardiness. According to Trey Naylor, the vine traveled from Europe to the United States and was planted at Bishop Lamy's rural retreat a few miles north of Santa Fe sometime in the 1850's. Bishop Lamy had arrived from France to oversee the newly created Southwest Catholic Diocese. A previous owner of the mercantile transplanted the vine from Santa Fe to its present location in the late 1960's. The land that comprises the vineyard was once part of a larger land grant that was ceded to settlers by the Spanish Crown in 1702.

"We think the mother vine is a Pinot Noir, but we don't know for sure," Trey Naylor said. "Rather than take a chance on planting cuttings from the mother vine, I purchased Pinot Noir vines."

"I planted the first vineyard entirely to Pinot Noir, because I was really interested in making wine from that grape," Trey explained. "The thin-skinned and finicky vinifera grows best in cool climates characterized by relatively short growing seasons." At an elevation of 5,700 feet, Jacona Valley's cool summer nights and brilliantly sunny days provide ideal conditions for growing outstanding Pinot Noir grapes, according to Naylor.

However, the weather in northern New Mexico did not fully cooperate. A cold winter and late spring frost in 2003 wiped out a good portion of the vines. Naylor was able to harvest enough grapes to produce his 2004 Estate Pinot Noir wine, which garnered a silver medal at the Southwest Wine Competition in Taos, New Mexico. Trey also lost many of the grapes to birds. He eventually resorted to netting all of his vines to keep the birds at bay. And, by 2007, he planted half of the vineyard to Baca Noir grapes, hoping they will be slightly hardier than the Pinot Noir.

Trey said he learns something every year he works with grapes. He enrolled in extension viticulture classes at the University of California, Davis, and used the services of a wine consultant before becoming a winemaker. He ferments the grape juice in insulated polyvinyl tanks. He uses a bladder press for removing the juice from the must and oak barrels for aging the wine.

Naylor discovered it worked best to use drip irrigation on the vines in the spring and summer, and then to flood irrigate the vines in the fall, and about once a month in the winter. He found that a soap and water spray works to control beetles on the vines.

"The help of other area winemakers has also been wonderful," Trey said. He's especially grateful to Jerry Burd of Black Mesa Winery for his assistance. He also receives help, especially at harvest time, from friends and neighbors. "I call them up the day before harvest and say 'be here' and they show up. We sometimes have around 70 people here picking grapes," he said.

It's not unusual for the Naylors to abide by Southern hospitality. Trey grew up in Alabama and Louisiana. He met his wife, Blair, while working on an offshore oil drilling operation. They have two children, 11-year-old Kate, and 8-year-old Thomas, who also help out in the vineyard. "It's really a labor of love for the entire family," Trey said.

Located a few miles north of Santa Fe, Jacona Valley Vineyards makes a fine side tour for visitors to the area. Eight Native American communities, called Pueblos, are located near Santa Fe. Early Spanish explorers established a community at the present site of Santa Fe, the capital city of New Mexico, planting the seeds of the Hispanic culture that still thrives there today.

Just as the Naylors lovingly care for the 150-year-old mother vine that grows between the old and new house, a Spanish-style residence built in 2007, they lovingly care for the new vines just down the driveway. Visitors can appreciate both old and new history at Jacona Valley Vineyards, in the highlands of northern New Mexico. ✳

A GIANT METAL BUTTERFLY SOARS ABOVE THE ROOFLINE
OF PONDEROSA WINERY IN PONDEROSA, NEW MEXICO.

A UNIQUE LICENSE PLATE ADORNS A TRUCK
AT PONDEROSA VALLEY WINERY.

PONDEROSA VALLEY WINERY
Ponderosa, New Mexico

Historian, mentor, wine doctor—these are some of the titles bestowed upon Henry Street—one of New Mexico's modern day wine pioneers. From Henry's viewpoint, luck played a part in the way those titles came to be associated with his name.

"It's always better to be lucky than good. We just happened to be in the right place at the right time," Henry says of the family's entry into the vineyard and wine business. Others will say it's Henry's willingness to help others and give back to the community that has made him one of the industry's most admired persons.

A love of the outdoors brought the Street family to Ponderosa, New Mexico, nearly forty years ago. Henry, Mary, and their four children began camping and fishing in the Ponderosa valley, where they found a weekend retreat from busy lives in the city. Henry worked as an engineer, at Sandia Laboratory in Albuquerque, for thirty years, before he turned the weekend retreat into a full-time business.

"We bought three acres in 1975, just to have for a campsite. I never thought I'd do anything else with that land," Henry said. "One of our sons, Kevin, had cerebral palsy. We found we could leave him at the camp with the dogs, where he had his freedom, while we went off hiking and fishing with the other kids. It was a grand time for the whole family."

However, Henry began wondering what else he might be able to do with the acreage he'd bought. He fondly recalled a trip he had taken to Switzerland, when he was stationed with the army in Germany. "They grew grapes there on those Swiss mountains, and I started to wonder if maybe I could grow grapes in the northern New Mexico mountains," he said.

At the same time, Mary saw a listing for a class on grape growing, sponsored by the University of New Mexico, in Albuquerque. Henry enrolled in the class, and, as the saying goes, the rest is history.

The Streets had the land leveled, with the help of the Soil Conservation Service, in 1976, and planted 500 vines with 24 varieties of grapes. Meanwhile, Henry was traveling to the West

Coast for his job, where he became friends with a California winemaker. The Californian told Henry that he ought to try growing Riesling grapes. Henry recruited his Sandia Lab buddies to help him bring back Riesling vine cuttings, on their many flights back and forth, from California to New Mexico. "The flight attendants would see us coming and joke, 'here come those Sandians with those sticks,'" he said.

Planting the Riesling grapevines proved to be a fortunate experiment, for they thrived in the high-altitude, red-rock canyons of northern New Mexico. Riesling grapes are the backbone of Ponderosa Valley Vineyards, with three quarters of the nine-acre vineyard containing them. Other varieties now include Pinot Noir, Baca Noir and Golden Muscat. The vines are watered from a drip irrigation system, with the water coming from the area's natural springs. Netting is placed over the ripening grapes to keep the birds from eating them, and Native American women, from nearby Jemez Pueblo, are hired to pick the grapes. After the harvest, grape stems and seeds are recycled, and mixed with cow manure, to fertilize the vineyard, where no chemical fertilizers are used.

Up until 1992, the grapes of Ponderosa Valley were made into wine by another New Mexico winery. Henry Street had decided he didn't want to have a winery, because some of the new wineries were struggling to find a market, though he did make some wine in his basement in Albuquerque. He joined the New Mexico Vine and Wine Society and helped sponsor the first wine festival in Bernalillo, in 1988.

A few years later, luck and skill boosted the Streets into their own winery business—Henry's garage-made wine won best of show, in the amateur category, at the 1992 New Mexico State Fair. It wasn't long before a winery building was constructed on the Ponderosa property.

Henry retired from Sandia Laboratory in 1994. The Streets moved to Ponderosa, built a home there, and opened the new winery. Henry became the winemaker, and Mary served as the business and tasting room manager. They produced 450 cases of wine the first year, with approximately 4,500 cases produced by 2007.

"I wanted to be known for the quality of my wines, so I set a standard, that each wine must win at least a bronze medal in a national competition, or it would not be sold," Henry said. The walls of the wood-paneled tasting room, festooned with colorful ribbons and shiny medals, show this goal has been achieved.

It took Henry several years to accumulate the necessary equipment for the winery. He started out with plastic fermentation tanks and gradually replaced some of them with stainless steel tanks. He also designed and built some equipment, and re-modeled a crusher/de-stemmer machine, so that the juice bins fit underneath the machine, rather than off to the side, as is the usual custom. Henry invested, with four partners, in a mobile bottling machine, in order to save the expense of purchasing one on his own. The device is mounted in a trailer and travels, periodically, to each of the partner's wineries, where 220 cases of wine can be bottled in three hours.

In addition to processing his own grapes, Henry buys grapes from other growers throughout New Mexico. The flagship wine of Ponderosa Valley Winery is the **New Mexico Riesling**, a sweet white wine made from 100 percent Ponderosa grapes; it has won numerous awards, including many gold medals. Other notable wines include **Tre Rossi**—a dry red wine with a full-bodied finish; **Jemez Red**—a semi-sweet red wine made from Ruby, Baco Noir, and Nebbiolo grapes; **Redondo Red**—a sweet red wine made from Ruby Cabernet, Leon Millot, Baco Noir, Pino Noir, and Vidal Blanc grapes; **Chenin Blanc**—a dry white wine, "crisp as a New Mexico morning;" and **Summer Sage**—a semi-dry white wine made from Golden Muscat, Vidal, Seyval and Riesling grapes. This is Mary Street's favorite wine and a favorite with visitors.

Henry Street prefers to craft dry wines, but he knows that in New Mexico, sweet wines are the best sellers. "My job is to sell wine, and sweet wine sales pay the bills," he said. By catering to the customers' needs, Henry has been able to place his wines in a major supermarket chain, several restaurants, and other retail outlets.

However, 80 percent of the wines are sold from the tasting room in Ponderosa. "We get a surprising amount of visitors here, around 27,000 per year," Henry said. The winery is located a few miles off of busy New Mexico Highway 4, which is a National Scenic Byway. Some of New Mexico's most gorgeous scenery and historic sites can be found along the route, including monumental red rock canyons, Jemez

Pueblo, the village of Jemez Springs, and Jemez State Monument. The Monument includes the ruins of a 14th century Indian pueblo as well as the ruins of a large 17th century Spanish mission.

Spanish explorers planted the first grapevines in New Mexico, making the state the oldest grape-growing region in the United States. Henry Street was intrigued by the Spanish influence in New Mexico, conducted research, and self-published a booklet—*The History of Wine in New Mexico, 400 Years of Struggle:*

> *In 1598—400 years ago, Don Juan de Onate led a small band of Spanish colonists from New Spain (now Mexico) northward, up the trail that would later be known as El Camino Real, to settle the fertile valleys of the upper Rio Grande. With the colonists came Franciscan monks to minister to their spiritual needs, and to bring the Holy Faith (Santa Fe) to the Indians. And they brought wine to celebrate their faith.*

MARY AND HENRY STREET POSE WITH DOGS, SAM, A GREAT PYRENEES, AND JACK, A SPRINGER SPANIEL, ON THE FRONT PORCH OF PONDEROSA WINERY.

The most important aspect of the Catholic faith is the celebration of the Eucharist at mass. Without exception, mass was celebrated every day by each Franciscan: central to the mass was wine, which represented the Blood of Christ. Only a small sip was required; however, it had to be wine...

A thousand miles and six months by ox-cart from the nearest source of this most vital product, kept future supplies constantly on the minds of the monks. Thus, the need for a reliable source of sacramental wine was the driving force for the initial development of the wine industry in New Mexico...

Spanish government officials, concerned about protecting revenues from the wine trade with the colonists, prohibited the raising of grapes in the New World...

This ban was in effect for over 150 years, however in the remote regions of the Spanish Empire, including northern New Mexico, the church chose to ignore the ban... and chose to resolve their problem by planting grapevines and making their own sacramental wine.

The first vines planted in what is now the state of New Mexico were brought in 1629 to Senecu, a Piro Indian pueblo south of Socorro, by Fray Gracia de Zuniga, a Franciscan, and Antonio de Arteaga, a Capuchin monk...the pueblo was slightly north of the present small village of San Antonio. The cuttings brought by the missionaries were a variety of Vitis vinifera, commonly called the "mission grape." Historians think it is a European variety from Spain, called Monica. This variety is still grown in New Mexico today.

Henry Street's book continues to outline the struggle for wine in New Mexico—the mission was attacked by Apache Indians in 1675, and in 1680, the Pueblo people revolted against Spanish masters, driving them out for several years. Spanish sovereignty was restored in 1692, and grapevines continued to flourish throughout New Mexico. By 1800, vineyards extended from El Paso, in the south, to Albuquerque, in the north, mostly along the Rio Grande River corridor. Wine was reported to be a major export by 1804, and continued to be a major industry well into the late 1800's.

However, by 1900, the wine industry in New Mexico started to decline, due to the entry of California into the market and weather-related problems. Prohibition, in 1919, further curtailed vineyards, though many families continued to produce wine in spite of the ban on legal production. In 1943, the greatest Rio Grande flood of the century destroyed vineyards throughout New Mexico's wine country, putting most growers out of business.

A new surge of vineyard activity began in 1980, when several groups of European investors rushed to plant large vineyards in New Mexico, lured by low-cost land and an expanding United States market. However, the new growers soon faced the realities of New Mexico's harsh winters and early spring frosts. They had also failed to develop a market for the huge quantities of wine being produced. Many of those vintners soon went out of business, but a few prevailed. Recognizing the need to promote the wine industry, people banded together to promote the wine festival concept. This proved to be successful and launched New Mexico's wine industry into today's successful enterprise.

Henry Street's foray into the New Mexico wine industry was not without its struggles. He often took some of his first wines to California, where experts there would help him analyze problems he had faced in making the wine. Henry brought this knowledge to his fellow New Mexico winemakers, by conducting seminars at state meetings, where he became known as the wine doctor. "Bring your wine you messed up, and we'll find out what it needs to fix or improve it," he tells other vintners.

Several winemakers join Henry at an annual harvest festival, held at El Rancho De Las Golondrinas, a living history museum, south of Santa Fe. They re-enact the process of making wine in the late 1800's, as described in Henry's book, from excerpts of reports by William M. Pierson, United States Consul in Ciudad Juarez, Mexico:

> *The wine manufacturer provided himself with a sufficient quantity of rawhide sacks, formed by fastening the outer edge of a large green hide to a sack form. The hide was then filled with water or dry sand, which stretched the hide into a sack like configuration...and allowed to dry until it was hard...tramping pans were set over the tops of the rawhide sacks...with holes to allow the juice of mashed grapes to drain into the sack...to extract the juice from the grapes, a person mashed the grapes with his feet while holding on to a brace or rope. The juice, fresh from the press, was poured into barrels and allowed to remain 10 days for hot fermentation...the juice was drawn off, leaving the sediment in the bottom of the barrel...then put in another barrel to ferment another 60 days...it was then cooled and left for 30 more days, when it was considered ready for use.*

Whether re-enacting the method of making wine in the 1800's, helping other winemakers to solve problems, or promoting New Mexico wine at a festival, Henry Street continues to serve as a mentor to his many peers. It's a lucky break for those who venture to Ponderosa Valley Vineyards and Winery on the southern slopes of the Jemez Mountains of northern New Mexico. ❧

JIM FISH DISPLAYS A WOODCARVING, WHILE STANDING IN FRONT OF AN ADOBE FIREPLACE, IN THE OPEN-AIR TASTING ROOM OF ANASAZI WINERY.

Anasazi Fields Winery
Placitas, New Mexico

On the western edge of the old village of Placitas, New Mexico, are orchards and vineyards watered by ancient spring-fed irrigation canals. The Anasazi, Native American peoples who lived there more than a thousand years ago, farmed the valley and left their petroglyph carvings on volcanic rock formations.

Spanish settlers founded the historic communal irrigation system, *acequias*, (Spanish for irrigation canal) that still support the culture and livelihood of thousands of New Mexico families. People continue to enjoy the culture and open space provided by life in the village of Placitas, Spanish for *Little Places*, situated north of Albuquerque and south of Santa Fe.

Jim Fish found this "little place" a perfect place to establish his winery, amongst acres of apricot, peach, cherry and plum orchards. Jim worked at Sandia Laboratories in Albuquerque, but found life in the village more suited to his lifestyle. He moved to Placitas in the 1980's, where he found time to enjoy the orchard, write poetry, carve wood, and brew a little beer.

A bumper peach crop in 1987 changed the focus of Jim's free time. "I decided to make a little peach wine, it was a big hit with my friends, and it somehow got out of control," he said.

Over the next several years, Jim made more and more wine from all the different fruits produced in his orchard. He opened the winery in 1995 with 400 gallons of bottled wine. He had another 10,000 gallons of wine aging in the cellar. Two years later he retired from his Sandia Lab position and devoted most of his time to the winery.

Jim Fish's approach to making non-grape fruit wines is somewhat different than most people expect. "At Anasazi Fields Winery we hand-craft dry table wines from fruits and berries other than grapes. Unlike most fruit wines, our wines are not sweet dessert wines. Their delicious dryness makes them the perfect accompaniment to any meal," he said.

What makes the Anasazi wines different is that they are fermented from the "whole fruit." The fruit is not peeled, pitted or crushed, but is put into the polyvinyl vats as whole fruit, where it is undergoes primary fermentation for three to six months. "I add sugar at the beginning, because grapes are the only fruit that has enough natural sugar to ferment on its own," Jim explained. "But as the fruit begins to ferment, I complete the process by using a cold, slow, sugar-starved fermentation. I also do not punch down the cap, as is the usual method when fermenting grape juice for wine," he added. The fruit juices are drained from the bottom of the mixture and then put into barrels with oak chips to age for several years. "All of my wines are aged for a minimum of three years, and some are aged as long as ten years."

Jim Fish says his wines are "intense, complex, bold, and evolving." He says the process has evolved over time and he is still exploring. "No commercial winemaker has ever been where I'm going with my fruit and berry wines. My partners and I are truly making the process up as we go."

Jim is the primary winemaker at Anasazi Fields Winery, though he has partners who helped to construct a winery and tasting room made from Ponderosa pine logs. The open construction of the building allows visitors the feeling of being outdoors, where they can enjoy the country fresh air; while, in the winter, a cozy corner fireplace provides added warmth.

Anasazi Fields Winery produces approximately 3,000 gallons of wine a year. The wines are bottled on a machine that is shared by four local winery operators, thus saving each individual the expense of owning expensive equipment. The machine is mounted in a trailer that is hauled to each winery when it's time to bottle wine.

The labels for Anasazi wines feature a cornstalk, because the orchard was once a field where the ancient Anasazi people raised corn. Each label also features a reproduction of petroglyph art found on rocks a short distance from the winery.

A primary goal of Anasazi Fields Winery is to help preserve the history and agricultural nature of the small villages of northern New Mexico by producing a value-added product from the excellent fruit grown there for centuries.

Jim Fish is also committed to producing wines that "reflect the unique landscape of artists and poets, weather and topography, science and magic." In addition to being the winemaker, Jim is an artist himself. He writes poetry and carves wood. Many of his carvings grace the winery, and are often made from the wood of trees that once grew in the orchard.

"I select a piece of wood to carve, based on shape and promise of interesting internal structure. From there, the process is organic and free flowing, as I follow the paths laid before me by the wood. I explore the interplay of positive and negative space to expose the natural beauty of the wood, and to create a sense of movement," Jim said.

Many events at Anasazi Fields Winery, often in conjunction with the village of Placitas, celebrate the artistic talents of local residents. Poetry readings, a solstice party, a harvest festival, and a holiday arts and crafts show are popular events. Spring is celebrated with the Placitas Studio Tour and a Fruits of the Earth Festival on Earth Day.

Jim Fish expresses his artistry in a poem titled "Waiting for Daybreak…"

> I sit here on the steps of the winery
> Waiting for daybreak
> Waiting for water to work its way
> Down
> Down the acequia
> Down thru the old village of Placitas
> Down past the houses of the newcomers
>
> Down past the big houses of the recent newcomers
> Down past the San Antonio Mission
> Down past the houses of the less recent newcomers
> The newcomers whose families
> Came with those who founded the Mission
>
> Down past the Presbyterian Church
> Down past the vineyards and orchards
> Down past the houses of those who never knew
> Or no longer hold irrigation a tradition
>
> Down past ancient fields
> Down an ancient acequia
> Down to an ancient Anasazi cornfield

And I
I sit
Surrounded by this ancient cornfield
Waiting
Waiting for water
Waiting for daybreak

Anasazi Fields Winery is open for free tastings and tours, Wednesday through Sunday from noon to 5 p.m. or by appointment. Visitors can taste several fruit wines including **New Mexico Apricot**—a rich, apricot wine with sherry overtones; **New Mexico Plum**—produced from 20 varieties of native plums; **New Mexico Peach**—a dry wine produced from select peaches grown in the Placitas area; **New Mexico Raspberry**—a big, rich and complex wine, with a balance of fruit and acid; and **New Mexico Rojo Seco**—one of the few wines blended with purchased wine. This wine is blended with a New Mexico grape wine, produced with stringent specifications by a southern New Mexico winery. The grape juice is blended with an older oak-aged fruit wine, put back on oak, and aged for two to three years before bottling.

Jim likes pairing wine with good food, though he considers pairing a personal preference. He and his friend, Dorothy Spencer, have published a book titled, *Culinary Suites and Solos*, with recipes and suggested menus for food and wine pairings.

"There is no future in being intimidated by the subject of pairing wines and food. If you like a particular wine with a particular dish, it works for you. If it does not work for one of your friends, save the pairing for friends for whom it does work," is Jim's philosophy. A suggested menu, from the cookbook, for a dinner for two includes Tiny Cheese Puffs, Salmon with Raspberry Wine, Scalloped Potatoes, Tossed Salad and Very Berry Pie.

Here is the recipe for Salmon with Raspberry Wine: Two, five-ounce salmon fillets; 6 tablespoons butter; 1 teaspoon green onion; 1 teaspoon fresh ginger; 4 tablespoons Anasazi Fields Raspberry Wine; 1 tablespoon lime juice; ½ cup champagne; 4 tablespoons clam juice or chicken broth; ¼ cup heavy cream, 3 tablespoons Chambord (raspberry liqueur). Dust fillets with flour and shake off excess. In a skillet heat butter and add salmon fillets. Brown slightly on one side and turn over. Add onion and ginger. With fillets still in the skillet, deglaze with raspberry wine, lime juice and champagne. Add fish or chicken stock and cream. Reduce until thickened. Add Chambord, cooking only until alcohol evaporates, 1 to 2 minutes. Serve garnished with fresh raspberries and lime zest.

A visit to Anasazi Fields Winery provides an experience found in only a few places in New Mexico. Guests can enjoy the fresh air and landscape while visiting with a master woodcarver, poet and winemaker. As Jim Fish says, "It's not a bad life." ❦

A SIGN WELCOMES VISITORS TO CASA RONDEÑA WINERY.

THE SPANISH STYLE GATE AND BUILDINGS WELCOME
VISITORS TO CASA RONDEÑA WINERY IN RANCHO DE LOS
ALBUQUERQUE. (COURTESY OF CASA RONDEÑA WINERY)

CASA RONDEÑA WINERY
Los Ranchos de Albuquerque, New Mexico

A rose-colored sunset washes over the land and showers the bell tower topping gray stone walls. It would be easy to imagine walking down a long row of grapevines, after working in the vineyard all day, coming home to a mansion in southern Spain. It would be equally easy to imagine hearing the strum of a Flamenco guitar, welcoming the vintner to dinner, by the fireplace in the great hall.

It's possible to make that imagination come to life by visiting Casa Rondeña Winery, in the village of Los Ranchos de Albuquerque, on the western edge of the city of Albuquerque. The owner and winemaker, John Calvin, his roots sown deep in the New Mexico soil, has created the vineyard and the Andalusian-inspired buildings, to reflect the Spanish heritage of New Mexico. Born in Los Ranchos de Albuquerque, Calvin became an architect, worked in several states, and traveled extensively in Europe before returning to New Mexico.

Calvin came to the winemaking industry in the 1990's, inspired by the influence of music, art and architecture. He feels that winemaking is a prime example of "a universal language unlike any other."

"Casa Rondeña Winery was a twinkle in my eye when I was studying and playing Flamenco guitar in southern Spain in the early 1970's," Calvin said. "As I studied the music in Andalusia and played the guitar, often into the wee hours of the morning, accompanying some of the great old Flamenco singers of the age, I was charmed by Roman, Arabic and other influence surrounding me."

As Calvin learned, Flamenco is a genuine Spanish art, existing in the forms of song, dance and guitar. Flamenco was influenced by gypsies and developed into an intense art form expressing deep feelings. Flamenco guitar, originally just a backdrop for the dancing and singing, became recognized as an art form in its own right. The most genuine Flamenco guitar music, some say, is experienced with a small group of friends around midnight, in southern Spain.

John Calvin learned to appreciate Flamenco guitar music in southern Spain, where he hung out with friends, enjoyed a glass of wine, and waited for someone to begin singing, so that he could play along on his guitar. He also learned to deeply appreciate the wine and the architecture.

He brought those influences home to his work in America, where he designed adobe houses. He also formed the philosophy that would guide him in establishing a winery. "I felt that in addition to music and architecture, growing grapes and making wine is another way to experience the beauty around us and to coax the diverse elements of nature and earth into a graceful fabric," he said.

In 1990, John and two of his young sons, Ross and Clayton, planted a vineyard on the present site of Casa Rondeña. They might well have been planting a vineyard where Spanish missionaries had grown grapes centuries earlier.

The first winemaking in New Mexico had stemmed from the need for sacramental wine after a number of missions were established in the Rio Grande River Valley of what was then called New Spain. Even though the Spanish Crown prohibited winemaking in the new territory that became New Mexico, the Franciscan monks smuggled in vines, planted them, and made wine. By 1885 New Mexico was the fifth largest wine producing area in the United States. However, California wine marketing, floods, and prohibition, eventually ended most of the production in New Mexico. New wineries began to emerge after World War II, but it was not until the 1980's that wine had its renaissance in New Mexico.

John Calvin opened Casa Rondeña winery to the public in 1998. He began with just one building which was also his home. The site was later expanded into several Spanish-style buildings, including a new home at the rear of the property, surrounded by bubbling fountains, ponds, trees and flower gardens. Events in the Great Hall, with its cathedral ceilings, antique oak fermentation tanks and Indian-carved sandstone-shaded windows, evoke a sense of grandeur. A new winery building, with a commemorative Tricentennial bell tower (celebrating the 300th anniversary of the founding of Albuquerque) completed the winery's expansion in the autumn of 2004.

The winery houses the French and American oak barrels where the red wines are aged, three stainless steel tanks for the white wines, an automated bottling line, a four-ton grape press, and a full chemistry laboratory. Grapes are grown in the vineyard next to the winery and at various locations throughout New Mexico.

Casa Rondeña's signature red wine is **Cabernet Franc**—the fruity style delivers black cherry, berry, light tobacco and chocolate flavors. The 2003 vintage won silver medals at the Southwest Wine Competition, the Florida International, and the Dallas Wine Competition. The 2004 vintage won gold at the American Wine Institute, and silver at the Riverside International Wine competition, the Tasters Guild International, Eastern Wine International, Jerry Mead's California competition, and the New Mexico State Wine competition.

Other notable wines include **Meritage Red**—a blend of Merlot, Cabernet Franc and Cabernet Sauvignon, this Bordeaux style red wine is gently aged in large hybrid oak barrels. It was a gold medal winner and named "Best Red in the Southwest" at the 2007 Taste of Taos Wine competition, in addition to winning medals at several other international contests; **Clarion**—a Spanish style red wine made from a blend of Syrah, Tempranillo and Cabernet Sauvignon grapes. It has an earthy texture, spicy middle and silky finish. It won gold at the New Mexico Wine competition; silver medals at Southwest Wine, California Critics Challenge, International Eastern Wine, and Tasters Guild International competitions; and bronze at a National Women's Wine contest; **Serenade**—a white wine blended from Riesling and Gewurztraminer grapes. It is an off-dry wine with lively, fruity flavors, winning a silver medal at the California Critics Challenge competition; and **Viognier**—a dry white wine with bright pineapple and apricot flavors. The 2006 vintage was a gold medal winner at the Hilton Head competition, the Florida State Fair, and the Tasters Guild International competition.

In addition to producing award winning wines, Casa Rondeña Winery is known as a center of gravity for culture in New Mexico. John Calvin tends the vines and wines with the same degree of respect and passion as his practices of music and architecture. He also feels that sharing wine is a way to bond with people.

"At Casa Rondeña, we will always include music, art, architecture, wine and philanthropy as our main focus," John emphasized. His wife, Christina Viggiano, whom he married in 2004, has aided him in that vision. "Her life in Italy and Italian heritage has brought a fresh passion, beauty and grace to the winery that is reflected in the wines and the grounds," he said.

WINTERTIME REFLECTIONS IN THE POOL AND GARDENS
ENHANCE THE BEAUTY OF THE LANDSCAPING
SURROUNDING CASA RONDEÑA WINERY.

"From humble but worthy roots to the 21st century new beginnings, the wine industry and wine making in Los Ranchos de Albuquerque has traveled an interesting and agriculturally challenging path in this beautiful land. The spirit of bringing forth not only the fruit of the vine but also the cultural flowering of the arts in New Mexico is the core of what I would like to bring to my neighbors and friends from near and far," Calvin added.

A walk through the vineyard, a visit to the tasting room, a stroll through the Great Hall and beyond to the fountains and gardens, brings a sense of majesty to the guest at Casa Rondeña. One is transported, in spirit, from New Mexico to Spain and home again, to a land of enchantment. ❦

TIERRA ENCANTADA VINEYARDS AND WINERY

Albuquerque, New Mexico

In a charming little corner of Albuquerque's South Valley, tucked between old adobe houses where chickens and geese roam backyard gardens, there is a modest wood-sided building holding a delicious surprise. A short drive from historic Old Town Albuquerque, and just off old Route 66, now Central Avenue, sits a small, family-owned winery, founded in 2005.

In one of the oldest agricultural regions of New Mexico, Jim Dowling and Pat Coil have named their winery *Tierra Encantada*. The name suits the area well, for the winery is located in the heart of land that was farmed for centuries by Native Americans, Spanish explorers, and other settlers. In Spanish, the name of the winery means *Enchanted Land*—"What better name for a winery located in New Mexico, known as the land of enchantment," said co-owner, Pat Coil.

Pat Coil, and her husband, Jim Dowling, produce estate bottled, single vineyard wines, from grapes grown in their ten-year-old San Vicente Vineyards. The vineyard is located 50 miles south of Albuquerque in Las Nutrias, New Mexico.

PAT COIL CALLS TO HER GEESE, AFLAC, LUCY, MOTHER AND SILLY, FROM THE FRONT PORCH OF THE TIERRA ENCANTADA WINERY IN ALBUQUERQUE, NEW MEXICO.

"The location of the vineyard, with well-drained sandy soil, is a great place to grow grapes," Pat said. "It's on a hillside on the side of Abbo Canyon, where the cold air drains down to the bottom of the hill. Since it's at 4,800 feet elevation, it helps to have the cold air move downward and not damage the tender grapevines," she added.

Jim Dowling is the vineyard manager and winemaker. He comes to the task from a lifetime of experience in one aspect or another of the wine industry.

As a young man living in Washington, D.C., Jim started tasting and collecting fine wines from the Bordeaux region of France. This led to studying about winemaking and great wine regions of the world. Eventually he planted his own small vineyard in Maryland, and gained his first experience in winemaking, using his own grapes.

A few years later Jim moved to New Mexico, where he worked as a scientist at the White Sands Missile Range near Alamogordo. After retirement, Jim and Pat moved to the Albuquerque area. He brings his scientific background to the operation of the winery, while Pat brings her business background to the facility.

Like most winemakers, Jim believes that you can't make good wine without good grapes. The vineyard is planted with mostly Rhone style grapes, and a few other varieties, including Syrah, Cabernet Sauvignon, Merlot, Mourvedre, Tempranillo, Viognier, White Muscat, Sauvignon Blanc, Chambourcin, Nebbiolo and Vidal.

Jim crafts the wine in small batches, producing 875 cases in 2007. He ferments the wine in stainless steel tanks and ages most of the red wines in French, American and Hungarian oak barrels. Pat says the New Mexico wine growers are passionate, enthusiastic, and help each other out, even though they are in competition with each other. "We give each other advice and sometimes share in buying and using equipment," she said.

"Henry Street of Ponderosa Vineyards has been a great mentor to all of us," Pat said. "He told me that I needed some 'froufrou' at the winery to amuse customers. So I got four geese and named them Aflac, Lucy, Mother and Silly. I'd say ninety percent of the people who visit the winery say they grew up with geese, and they often have great goose stories to share."

After the winery geese greet them, visitors can enter the tasting room, decorated in Art Nouveau style. The walls are painted with colorful murals, enhancing the beauty of the antique tin ceiling. The carved wood bar, circa 1900, was purchased on e-Bay and shipped to New Mexico from Minnesota.

Guests are often served wine by Pat Coil, or one of her many volunteers. "We are very fortunate to have wonderful volunteers. I teach them the basics of wine in a five-hour class and then they work for us. They help us through the entire process of winemaking, including bottling and labeling. They give us great advice, often get our wines into stores, and bring their friends to the winery. We couldn't do without them."

The winery's best selling wine is **Chambourcin**, a blend of Chambourcin and Cabernet Sauvignon grapes. It won silver medals at the Southwest Wine and California Women's Wine competitions and a bronze medal at the Indy State Fair. The **Cabbiolo** wine is a blend of Cabernet Sauvignon, Cabernet Franc and Nebbiolo grapes. **Atrisco Sunset** is a sweet red wine that has the taste of chocolate covered cherries. **Dessert Muscat** is a white wine with a floral nose. **Tempranillo** is a dry red wine with flavors of blackberry, spice, and tobacco that won a silver medal at the Southwest Wine competition. **Merlot** is Pat Coil's personal favorite wine, a complex, full-bodied red wine that won a bronze medal at the Southwest Wine competition.

Although Pat, Jim, and the volunteers prefer to host visitors at the winery, it's possible to meet them and learn about their wines at many festivals. Some of these events include the Southern New Mexico Wine Festival in Las Cruces and the Albuquerque Wine Festival in Albuquerque on Memorial Day weekend; the Santa Fe Wine Festival in Santa Fe on the Fourth of July weekend; the New Mexico Wine Festival at Bernalillo, the Wine Lifestyle Expo in Albuquerque and the Harvest Festival in Las Cruces, all on Labor Day weekend.

The hosts at Tierra Encantada Winery also encourage visitors to explore other sights in the Albuquerque area. Petroglyph National Monument includes dormant volcanoes, archeological sites and an estimated 20,000 carved images produced by Native Americans. There are several nearby Native American Pueblos. Old Town Plaza

PAT COIL, CO-OWNER OF
TIERRA ENCANTADA WINERY IN
ALBUQUERQUE, NEW MEXICO,
DISPLAYS A FEW OF HER
AWARD-WINNING WINES.

and the Hispanic Cultural Center, focusing on the Spanish heritage of Albuquerque, provide historical information. A trail of vintage neon signs on old Route 66 has been restored to its former glory. The University of New Mexico campus is easily accessible. The world's largest hot air balloon event, the Albuquerque International Balloon Fiesta, is held during the first full week of October.

Centuries of history have shaped the character of Albuquerque. Starting with the Native Americans, who have lived there for thousands of years, and continuing through Albuquerque's official founding in 1706 by Spanish settlers, the city has grown into a multi-cultural metropolis. Arts and crafts, music and culture, are all part of the landscape of this central New Mexico city. It lies a mile above sea level and has a high-desert climate, guarded by the 10,600 foot peaks of the Sandia Mountains on the eastern side. Sandia means *watermelon* in Spanish, and it's said that anyone who has seen the setting sun splash pink light over the rocky peaks knows exactly how they earned the name.

From the eastern mountains to the southwest plains, or near the Rio Grande River flowing through Albuquerque, visitors are sure to find excitement or peace and quiet somewhere along the way. Tucked into a corner that was once a farmer's field is Tierra Encantada Winery, a truly enchanting place in New Mexico. ❧

Tularosa Vineyards
Tularosa, New Mexico

Spanish settlers, who gave it a colorful name, founded the village of Tularosa, in southeastern New Mexico, in 1862, along the banks of the Rio Tularosa. A vineyard also adopted the same name more than a hundred years later.

Tularosa comes from the Spanish description for the red or rose-colored reeds the settlers found growing along the banks of the river. The village today remains much the same as it was when it was founded—it has been declared a historic district, and placed on the National Register of Historic Places.

The Spanish settlers brought grapevine cuttings of Mission vines with them to plant on their farms. The farms were irrigated by *acequias*, ancient ditch watering systems that brought water from the nearby Rio Tularosa. Today, the original *acequias* remain, virtually

DAVID WICKHAM DISPLAYS SOME OF THE WINE BARRELS USED TO AGE WINE AT TULAROSA VINEYARDS.

unchanged, providing the water for the tree-lined streets, private gardens, and village landscapes.

David Wickham moved to Tularosa a little more than 100 years after the first Mission grapes had been planted there. Eventually, he also grew Mission grapes, and named a vineyard with the same name as the town. He had married a native girl, Teresita Chavez, when he was stationed at nearby Holloman Air Force Base, ten years earlier. After tours of duty in Germany and Turkey, the couple returned to Tularosa in 1976 where David gardened and grew fruit trees on a half-acre lot, a gift from his in-laws.

"There were a few Mission grapes on my lot, and I noticed other grapes growing in yards around town. I learned that vineyards had flourished there in the past, and I wondered why more grapes weren't being grown at the present time," David said.

David had enjoyed the wines in Germany when he was stationed there, and that piqued his interest in the possibility of planting a vineyard and making wine. He enrolled in classes at New Mexico State University in Alamogordo, while working again at Holloman Air Force Base. A college research paper he completed, on the history of growing grapes in New Mexico, was the catalyst for planting his own vineyard.

Wickham's research included this item from the September 1932 issue of *The Alamogordo News*:

> In 1870, Tularosa had grown in population to nearly a thousand souls…five or six hundred acres were farmed with Tularosa river water. Grapes were planted and wine was made to supply the local requirements.

"I ordered a few grapevines from a catalog, just to see how they would grow in my little garden," David said. "They did great and I started making wine in my basement. Two years later, I attended several grape growing and winemaking seminars sponsored by the New Mexico Vine and Wine Society. I really caught the bug then. I wanted to buy more land and plant a real vineyard."

While searching for land near Tularosa, David often drove by a small farm north of town on his way to obtain gravel. "I'd stop and visit with the owner because we both liked to garden. After a while he told me he'd like to sell his land and we made a deal. The farm had

MAX, THE WINERY DOG, RECEIVES ATTENTION FROM DAVID WICKHAM AT TULAROSA VINEYARDS AND WINERY. MAX RECEIVES TIPS FROM CUSTOMERS, AND HIS PRESENCE IS REQUESTED BY RETURN VISITORS TO THE WINERY.

been planted to pecan trees, some of which we kept. There was also a lot of mesquite and creosote bush to be cleared before I could plant a vineyard," he said.

Finally, in 1985, Tularosa Vineyards became a reality, when David planted 150 Merlot and Grenache grapevines. The following year he added 500 vines, including Chenin Blanc, Sauvignon Blanc and Cabernet varieties. Later he added the varieties of Sangiovese and Tempranillo. He continued to grow Mission and Black Muscat grapes on the town property, where he maintained his home.

David installed a drip irrigation watering system at the farm, getting the water from a shallow well, rather than the *acequias* system. "Drip irrigation allows grape farmers to control the quality of the grapes, by not over watering, as well as conserving water. This is achieved by controlling the water within the root zone of the grapevines. Grapevines use significantly less water than other water-intensive crops like alfalfa and pecans," he explained.

Wickham also encouraged other farmers in the Tularosa Basin to plant grapes, and he purchases grapes from some of them for the wines of Tularosa Winery. "This is an ideal grape-growing area," he said. "In the summer growing season our daytime temperature can reach the upper 90's, but the night time temperature often drops dramatically to the upper 50's. This tremendous diurnal shift is what gives wine grapes bold flavors and good acid. Without this cooling influence the wines would be flat and insipid, and without the sunlight the wines would be extremely acidic," David explained.

The winemaking facility, built next to the farm vineyard, has a capacity to produce up to 10,000 gallons of wine each year. The harvested grapes are processed with a mechanical de-stemmer/crusher, and the juice is pressed through a German- manufactured wine press. Fermentation is done mostly in polyvinyl tanks. All red wines are aged in oak barrels.

The process of making wine today is a far cry from the way it was made in 1870, as described in 1932, by *The Alamagordo News*:

> The usual method of manufacture was very primitive and crude...the grapes were emptied into rawhide containers, sack like affairs suspended on forked posts...men in their bare feet tramped the grapes to a pulpy mass, sinking to their knees in the process. The crushed grapes were then allowed to stand in the hide sacks until hot fermentation was complete...after ten days the fermented juice was dipped into other vats and cool fermentation was allowed to complete the process. The wine was then placed in small barrels for 30 days. Some wines were a well-flavored stimulating beverage, while others made a vinegar-like product that intoxicated and sickened with a nauseating flavor.

Nearly 150 years later, Tularosa Vineyards is producing high quality, international award-winning wines, in their modern facility. David Wickham's son, Chris, is now the winemaker, taking over in 1995. Chris worked at the winery during his college years while he earned a degree in International Marketing.

Visitors are invited to enjoy the award-winning wines of Tularosa Vineyards at the facility, two miles north of the historic village of Tularosa. Tularosa is nestled at the bottom of the Sacramento

Mountains and is the gateway to the mountain resort village of Ruidoso, the Mescalero Indian reservation, and the Lincoln National Forest. It is also only minutes away from the White Sands National Monument, where great wave-like dunes of gypsum sand have engulfed 275 square miles of desert, and created the world's largest gypsum dune field.

At Tularosa Vineyards picnic tables are available under the pecan trees, next to the attractive tasting room, or visitors may enjoy relaxing on the covered redwood deck, attached to the front of the building. Max, the friendly winery dog, a white Great Pyrenees, often greets guests. Max has earned tips from customers, who ask to see him on their return visits to the winery.

Some of the wines that may be enjoyed from the Tularosa Vineyards winery include **Viognier, Cabernet Sauvignon, Billy's Blush, Muscat Cannelli**, and **Symphony**. The wine bottles, fittingly, are graced with labels featuring a painting of a rose, because David Wickham says that the rose is also a symbol for Tularosa.

Tularosa wines can also be sampled at several of the annual New Mexico wine festivals throughout the state. Father and son load up a trailer, filled with wine, tables and coolers, and head off to the festivals "just like circus guys," David said. ❧

A SIGN WELCOMING VISITORS TO HEART OF THE DESERT VINEYARDS NEAR ALAMOGORDO, NEW MEXICO.

THIS NEW VINEYARD WAS PLANTED IN 2008 AT HEART OF THE DESERT VINEYARDS NEAR ALAMOGORDO, NEW MEXICO.

HEART OF THE DESERT VINEYARDS
Alamogordo, New Mexico

Sky, space, sunsets, and stars are among the attributes that convinced the Schweers family to choose the Tularosa Basin of New Mexico as a working retirement home. They had once lived in New Mexico, and then in other places, including tropical Hawaii, so it was quite a contrast to return to the desert.

George Schweers, an Air Force officer, was stationed, at various times, at Holloman Air Force Base, near Alamogordo. He had grown up in rural Nebraska and had always set a goal of returning to agriculture after military service. George's wife, Marianne, shared the dream of having a farm, but she was unsure about the New Mexico landscape. "I thought I'd never seen anything so bare as the desert. But, each time we came back to New Mexico, it looked better," she said. "I learned to appreciate the open spaces and felt like I was in tune with the world when I was in the desert. Most of all, the warmth of the people convinced me to make New Mexico home."

George, Marianne, and their children, Gordon, Laura, and Jean began a research project to see what plants would grow in the desert. The research provided the name of pistachio trees as a viable crop. As it happened, a friend had planted 400 pistachio trees near Alamogordo. When the friend's job there ended, in 1974, he sold his farm to the Schweers. George still had five years left until retirement from the Air Force.

"Little did we know what was in store for us," Marianne said. For the first five years, George, Marianne and the children did all the farming. "We were at the farm after work, after school and on weekends. One year we planted another 700 trees with the help of Gordon's high school baseball team, who agreed to help as a way to raise funds for the team."

There were many challenges for the family in establishing the Eagle Ranch Pistachio Groves. Additional challenges came along, when they added the Heart of the Desert Vineyards, a few years later.

"Being the only pistachio grove in New Mexico, there was no support industry for harvesting or processing," Marianne said. They developed their own processing operation, making or buying equipment. Today, the pistachio farm, now with 12,000 trees on 85 acres, is totally self-contained. Daily field care, harvesting, processing, and marketing the finished product is completed on the local farm.

Because it takes four years for a pistachio tree to produce nuts, and an alternate crop was needed in case the trees didn't produce at all in some years; the Schweers searched for other crops that would grow well in the desert. They decided to try grapes and established Heart of the Desert Vineyards. In the spring of 2003, they planted 12,000 vines of Chardonnay, Cabernet Sauvignon, Shiraz and Zinfandel grapes, on nine acres. The vineyards were expanded in 2005 with the planting of four more acres with Malvasia Bianca, Gewurztraminer, and Riesling vines. "It takes at least three years for grapes to mature, so I'm not sure we changed things much, but at least if one crop failed, perhaps we'd get production from the other one," Marianne said. Indeed the entire cash crop of pistachios was lost to a freeze in 2007.

The Heart of the Desert vineyard is a work in progress. The Schweers have been contracting with another New Mexico winery, to have the grapes made into wine for sale at their farm tasting room. They also sell grapes to other wineries. Plans are to open a new winery, tasting room and events center in 2009.

Busy New Mexico highway 54-70 cuts directly through the middle of the two agricultural enterprises. Eagle Ranch Pistachio Groves, both the tree groves and the retail outlet, are situated on the west side of the highway. Heart of the Desert Vineyards is located on the east side of the highway. The new winery, tasting room and events center will be located next to the vineyard, with a grand view of the Sacramento Mountains to the east.

"We get many, many visitors, who stop in while traveling the highway that passes our store," Marianne said. She said the road is traveled by hundreds of commercial vehicles each day, by residents of Alamogordo, and by people stationed at Holloman Air Force Base. Tourists also drive by, while visiting the nearby

White Sands National Monument, or headed to the mountain resort town of Ruidoso.

Alamogordo was founded in 1898 as a terminal for the railroad. Holloman Air Force Base is the area's largest employer. The base is the home of the F-117 Stealth Fighter Wing, the German Air Force in the U.S., and the High Speed Test Track. White Sands Missile Range is the testing site for the U.S. rocket program and other research and evaluation programs.

White Sands National Monument is a major tourist attraction. Rising from the heart of the Tularosa Basin, it is one of the world's great natural wonders. Great, wave-like dunes of gypsum sand cover 275 square miles, where plants and animals have successfully adapted to the constantly changing environment.

Visitors to the area will find it well worth the time and effort to pay a visit to Eagle Ranch Pistachio Grove and Heart of the Desert Vineyards. The tasting room, complete with gift shop and artist gallery, is open Monday through Saturday from 8 a.m. to 6 p.m. and Sunday from 9 a.m. to 6 p.m. Farm tours are also offered daily.

The signature wine at Heart of the Desert combines the flavors from both sides of the Schweers farm, pistachio nuts and grapes. **Pistachio Rose** is a blend of red and white grapes, Zinfandel and Chenin Blanc, with the subtle nutty flavor of pistachios.

Marianne Schweers's favorite wine is **Viva La Roja**—a blend of three classic grapes for a rich, sweet, full-bodied wine. Other wines include **Cabernet Sauvignon**—made from premium, red wine grapes, a dry wine with the taste of dark cherry, cedar and black current; **Chardonnay**—a classic white wine, medium dry; **Merlot**—a wine with berry bouquet and a soft, fruity, smooth texture; **Muscat of Alexandria**—a sweet, very floral dessert wine; and **Syrah**—a rich wine with intense color and flavor.

The welcome mat is always out at the Schweers farm and vineyard. Warmed by a golden sun, the groves and vineyards of a thriving family farm are sure to warm the heart and soul of those who venture to find such delights in the desert. ❧

The front entrance to La Viña Winery, the oldest modern-day winery in New Mexico.

A sign welcomes visitors to La Viña Winery.

La Viña Winery

La Union, New Mexico

Centuries of history are found along the trail leading to La Viña Winery, in the southeast corner of New Mexico. It's only a skip away from the Mexico border, and a hop away from Texas.

Visitors can traverse part of the Don Juan de Oñate trail, on Highway 28, south of Las Cruces, which leads to New Mexico's oldest winery. Don Juan de Oñate arrived in the area, near the Rio Grande River, in 1598, after struggling for months to bring his large caravan of people and animals north from Mexico. The trail became known as the El Camino Real, the Royal Road, and was for some time the longest European road in North America.

Ken and Denise Stark traveled part of this same trail, in the late 1980's, in search of a vineyard. The Starks had been farming and ranching in the Texas Panhandle, but wanted to make a change. They spent a month traveling from Texas to California, searching for a perfect place. They ended up in Albuquerque for a few years, where Ken worked as the assistant winemaker for Anderson Valley Vineyards, and later became the winemaker there.

"I had a good agricultural background, had taken wine appreciation classes, and I had a good palate for tasting wine," Ken said. He worked for Anderson until 1992, when he got an offer to work for a winery in El Paso, Texas, that he felt he couldn't refuse. The El Paso owner, Dr. Clarence Cooper, also owned the La Viña Winery in New Mexico, which had been established in 1977 by Cooper. The Starks bought La Viña in 1993, and "found the perfect place they'd been looking for."

The original vineyard of 14 acres was north of the present facility. The Starks needed more land and a larger production area, so they purchased a larger acreage and moved the vineyard and winery five miles to the south.

"When we bought the new property, there were 44 acres of jalapeno peppers and nine acres of pecan trees. We cleared most of that land and planted 24 acres of vines with 22 varieties of grapes," Ken said.

A few acres of pecan trees remain, but the remainder of the orchard was turned into a parking lot. The vineyard was planted to mostly Rhone and Italian varieties of grapes, including Syrah,

KEN STARK, CO-OWNER AND WINEMAKER AT LA
VIÑA WINERY, PREPARES TO HOST A WINE TASTING
AT THE WINERY NEAR LA UNION, NEW MEXICO.

Cabernet, Merlot, Chardonnay, Primitivo, Muscat, Riesling, Viognier, and Zinfandel. By 2007, the vineyard produced 160 tons of grapes. Some of the grapes are sold to other wineries, with the balance made into 3,000 cases of wine each year at La Viña Winery.

The state of the art winery is equipped with steel fermenting tanks, a crusher, bladder press, automated bottling machine, and 100 French oak barrels. There are several employees who work in the vineyard and winery, including an assistant winemaker.

"We make 80 percent of our product as sweet wine and 20 percent is dry wine. Most of our customers come from El Paso and they like sweet wines," Ken said.

One of Ken's goals is to have the Mesilla Valley recognized as an American Vineyard Appellation area. He says it's a good grape growing area, with sandy loam soil, and an average temperature near that found in Paso Robles, California, a prime vineyard area.

Denise Stark serves at the business and tasting room manager. Almost all of the wine produced at La Viña Winery is sold directly to customers from the tasting room, or at events and festivals hosted by La Viña.

Stone arches, directing visitors to the large open space areas that are used for special events, surround the Spanish style stone winery and tasting room. The spacious grounds are available for weddings, picnics and other events. La Viña hosts a Blues and Jazz Festival in April, an old-fashioned country picnic and open house on July 4th, and a Harvest Festival and Grape Stomp each year in October. These festivals often bring from four to nine thousand visitors to the winery.

"We don't attend the state festivals anymore," Ken said. "We've done all the standing in a tent all day long that we ever want to do." More than 400 volunteers assist the Starks in producing their events.

Some of the wines available to visitors at La Viña Winery include **Viognier**—a dry white wine aged in oak barrels; **Syrah**—a dry red wine with a toasty oak aroma; **Rojo Loco**—crazy red wine, made from a blend of Cabernet and Zinfandel grapes, some liken it to Sangria; **Oro Loco**—crazy gold wine, made from a Muscat blend with citrus notes; **La Dolce Viña**—sparking Muscat wine, the best selling wine at La Viña; and **La Piñata**—sparkling wine made from a blend of black Muscat and white Zinfandel, its referred to as a party in a bottle.

It's a short drive to La Viña Winery from Las Cruces, New Mexico, or El Paso, Texas. Starting from Las Cruces, visitors can travel south, through the historic Spanish village of Mesilla, following Highway 28; they will be traveling approximately the route of the historic Don Juan de Oñate trail.

The trail today meanders past pecan groves and fields of chile and cotton. Six miles south of Mesilla is the world's largest family-owned pecan farm. Stahmann Farms has 180,000 trees and produces from 8 to 10 million pounds of pecans annually.

Visitors coming from El Paso will travel north on I-10, taking Exit 2 in Texas. From there they follow Vinton Road a few miles west to the winery. Once the hustle and bustle of the busy interstate is left behind, the peace and quiet of farm country still abides in the far southeast corner of New Mexico.

La Viña Winery, meaning *The Vineyard* in Spanish, is a place to relax and enjoy life. From the welcoming arched gateway, to the warm wood interior of the tasting room, visitors feel like they have stepped back in time. More than four hundred years earlier, the people in Don Juan de Oñate's caravan may have relaxed at this same spot. ❧

THE TASTING ROOM AT SOUTHWEST WINES,
FORMERLY KNOWN AS ST. CLAIR WINERY.

A STATE-OF-THE-ART BOTTLING MACHINE AT SOUTHWEST
WINERY IN DEMING, NEW MEXICO, FILLS, CORKS AND LABELS
THOUSANDS OF BOTTLES OF WINE IN A FEW HOURS.

STARLEY TALBOTT

SOUTHWEST WINES
Deming, New Mexico

The Lescombes family brought with them to America the necessary ingredients for a renaissance—renewal, rebirth, revival of art and learning—to the desert of New Mexico. The state's largest winery preserves the family traditions transferred from Europe.

When Herve Lescombes left France, as the fifth generation winemaker at Domaine de Perignon Winery in Burgundy, he brought his family to New Mexico. He selected New Mexico because its hot dry desert days, cool nights, and sandy soil was similar to his native Algeria. Lescombes founded Blue Teal Vineyards in 1981 and opened the family's St. Clair Winery in 1984. At that time, a number of European investors had planted around 7,000 acres of grape vines in southern New Mexico, where they learned wine grapes had flourished hundreds of years earlier. Most of those vineyards eventually failed, due to weather and marketing problems, but the Lescombes family prevailed.

The present manager of the business, now called Southwest Wines, Florent Lescombes, was 11 years old when he came with his family to New Mexico. He and his brother, Emmanuel, grew up with the business and are now the primary operators. Emmanuel is the vineyard manager, with 200 acres of grapes to tend, near Lordsburg, New Mexico. Florent took over as the chief winemaker, but now devotes more time to management, and employs a winemaker.

"My father left France because the regulations for operating a vineyard and winery there are very strict," Florent said. "Here, in America, it is much easier to be creative with what you can do in the vineyard and winery."

French wine laws set rigid rules on making wine including: the location and size of the vineyard, the variety of grape, yield per hectare, vineyard practices, winemaking practices, level of alcohol in the wine, amount of wine produced, and labeling. Burgundy is a small wine region in central eastern France, with thousands of tiny vineyards, often having multiple owners for each vineyard.

The Lescombe family was happy to be rid of the complex French wine laws. However, they brought one firm belief with them—"the heart of the business is the vineyard," Florent said. "The land itself determines what the grapes and the wine will become. Many things define the *terroir*—soil, slope, elevation, sun and moisture are some of the components. In French there is no word for winemaker, because nature makes the wine. In Burgundy, the name used to describe a vintner is *vigneron*, which means grape grower," he explained. "That is why Emmanuel has the most important job, as the vineyard manager. Wine is a food product and you cannot have good wine without good fruit."

The current winemaker at Southwest Wines, Philippe Littot, also from France, echoes that sentiment. "Winemaking is easy," he said, "you just need good quality grapes to begin with."

Southwest Wines makes 40 to 60 different types of wines, including contracting for other vineyards and wineries, producing thousands of gallons of wine in the Deming facility.

Philippe describes the process of making wine—"for the white wines, we crush and de-stem the grapes, then we put the mixture in the bladder press. We press the juice out very slowly, trying not to break the skins. The juice is then pumped into a stainless steel tank and cooled right away. It is left for one or two days, so that any residue will fall to the bottom. When the juice is clear, the pH, sugar and acidity levels are tested, and the juice is moved to another tank. Depending on the style of wine that is desired, yeast will be added to begin the fermentation process. Yeast turns the sugar to alcohol during fermentation. We stop the fermentation, depending on what style of wine is being made, sweet, semi-sweet, or dry."

"For red wines, the grape skins are left on during fermentation. They are often left to ferment for five days up to two weeks. The red wines are usually aged one year in oak barrels and six months in the bottle," Philippe said.

A new technique is being tried at Southwest Wines, called micro-oxygenation. Philippe explained it is the process of "introducing a small amount of oxygen, about two milliliters per liter of wine, into the tank, each month, while the wine is fermenting. We use oak chips in the tank, so that we are mimicking the process of aging wine in an oak barrel. It's a very precise process and I must be careful not to put in too much oxygen too quickly, or the wine could become spoiled.

The advantage of this technique is that we would not have to buy so many new oak barrels. We'll see how it works out."

After the grapes are de-stemmed and crushed, the leftover stems and seeds are mixed with animal fertilizer and spread back onto the vineyard. The vineyard, at an elevation of 4300 feet, has a mixture of sandy soil and is watered with a drip irrigation system. "It's taken us twenty years to understand the soil and climate at the vineyard, and how best to grow grapes there," Florent said.

New vines for the vineyard are cultivated by taking cuttings from the old vines during winter and spring pruning. The cuttings are placed in soil and kept in a nursery for several months until they form a root system. They are then placed in sawdust for two to three months to keep them from germinating, until they can be planted in March or April of the next year. The vines are planted five feet apart in rows eight feet apart, allowing around 1000 vines per acre. The main varieties are Cabernet Sauvignon, Chardonnay, Sauvignon Blanc, and Zinfandel.

The New Mexico climate is considered to be ideal for growing grapes, according to Florent. "There is a forty degree temperature difference between day and night in the summer, just what grapes love. We have an abundance of sunshine, so that causes the ripening grapes to produce plenty of sugar."

Unlike most small vineyards in New Mexico, the bulk of the grapes at Southwest Wines are harvested by machine, during the cool of the night. They are trucked immediately to the winery in Deming. They are made into many different wines under several different labels resulting in more than 70,000 cases of wine annually.

Approximately 15,000 visitors stop by the tasting rooms of Southwest Wines each month. Wine tastings are available in Deming, Las Cruces and Albuquerque. Guests may try many different wines including **Blue Teal Muscat**—a white, Mediterranean style wine, with a floral aroma; **Blue Teal Shiraz**—a full-bodied velvety red wine with hints of ripe berries; **D.H. Lescombes Chardonnay**—a white wine with a semi-sweet, vanilla flavor; **D.H. Lescombes Syrah**—a red wine with black pepper and cherry aromas; **D.H. Lescombes Royal Kir**—a semi-sweet sparkling wine; **St. Clair Malvasia Bianca**—a rich white dessert wine with tropical fruit flavors; **St. Clair Nebbiolo**—a semi-sweet red wine with a fruity aroma; **St. Clair Cab-Zin**—a full-bodied red wine, made from a blend of

FLORENT LESCOMBES, A SIXTH-GENERATION MEMBER OF A WINEMAKING FAMILY FROM FRANCE, POURS A GLASS OF WINE AT SOUTHWEST WINERY.

Cabernet Sauvignon and Zinfandel grapes; and **St. Clair Bellissimo**—a sweet Muscat sparkling wine, similar to Italian spumante.

New Mexico specialty wines—**Plum-Loco**, a sweet red wine with black cherry and plum flavors; **Wine-A-Rita**, a sweet margarita wine with the tangy taste of lime; and **Green Chile Wine**, a wine highlighting New Mexico green chile—are also popular.

Southwest Wines have garnered multiple awards for their wines including an amazing ten silver medals in one competition, the 2008 Houston Livestock Show and Rodeo International Wine Competition. Southwest Wines participates in several New Mexico wine festivals each year, and their wines are available at numerous retail outlets throughout the state. There is also dining available at the St. Clair Winery and Bistros in Albuquerque and Las Cruces.

Dozens of people, including extended family members, are responsible for making Southwest Wines the largest winery in New Mexico, and keeping the operation running smoothly. Florent and Emmanuel Lescombes say they couldn't be successful without such devoted assistance.

The brothers, modern day renaissance men, are carrying on the family's six-generation history of winemaking. But, as the saying goes in Burgundy, "*Laissez le vin de se faire:* Let the wine make itself." ❧

ARIZONA

ROWS OF GRAPEVINES LIE DORMANT IN FEBRUARY AT COLIBRI VINEYARD IN SOUTHEASTERN ARIZONA.

A VIEW OF COLIBRI VINEYARDS.

STARLEY TALBOTT

COLIBRI VINEYARD AND WINERY
Portal, Arizona

E very facet of Bob Johnson's senses was fine-tuned that April day, in 1995, when he first trod a piece of land on the northeast slopes of the Chiricahua Mountains in southeast Arizona. He smelled the fragrance of bursting blossoms on hundreds of apple trees, he felt a gentle breeze on his skin, he heard creek water bubbling over stones, he tasted the pungency of pine, he touched a handful of the limestone soil, and he gazed at the amazing scenery surrounding him.

"As I walked this land I felt it call to me, there were signs everywhere," Johnson said. After living and working for several years with Native Americans he had learned to appreciate the feeling of a spirit or a force present around him. "While I stood surveying the buildings and grounds, my gaze was suddenly drawn to a hilltop overlooking the entire site. There, at the crest of the hill was a perfect stone arch, carved thousands of years ago by the combined forces of nature. Native Americans believe that the stone arch, this frozen rainbow, is a sign, a calling, and a good luck charm. Without hesitation I phoned my wife and asked her to come visit our new retirement home," Johnson recalled.

His wife, Michelle McDonald, a busy Tucson doctor, heeded the call and fell in love with the place, too. The couple, along with their three children, purchased the property and set to work creating their dream retirement home. Although Michelle and the children retained their home in Tucson and continued to work and attend school there, they helped Bob with the new purchase and have "enjoyed many fine days and weeks there."

Johnson determined that most of the apple trees would have to be removed, because he wanted to plant a vineyard. He said the deer and bear loved to raid the old apple orchard, planted by Ralph Morrow, which had been neglected for several years. There was an abandoned silver mine, dating back to the 1850's, on a steep hillside above the orchard. Morrow had moved the former mine manager's house down from the mine to a site near the orchard.

BOB JOHNSON PRUNES VINES IN FEBRUARY AT HIS COLIBRI VINEYARD IN SOUTHEASTERN ARIZONA.

The property has a virtually limitless supply of water, because the old mine shaft had been flooded with water from mountain springs. The original owners had piped the water down the hill from the mine. They established a pre-statehood water right that still flows to this day. Johnson added a storage tank above the vineyard and created a secluded fishing pond surrounded by shade trees. The water is piped by gravity flow to nourish the vineyard by means of a drip irrigation system.

After the land was cleared, the site was planted with seven varieties of wine grapes including Syrah, Grenache, Mourvedre, Counoise, Roussanne, Viognier and Petit Verdot. Johnson explained these grape varieties are found most commonly in the Rhone Valley of France.

Johnson began a soil restoration project by bringing in tons of hay and manure. He also planted native grass seeds as a cover crop. The elevation at the top of the vineyard's north facing slope is 5,300 feet; and the land slopes down to 5,225 feet near the bottom of the vineyard, where the winery is located. Johnson said there is constant wind movement through the vineyard helping to keep the temperature moderate during the day and discourage insects. He said the moderate daytime temperatures revert to colder night temperatures, providing a wide temperature range, considered the ideal climate for grapes.

A vertical shoot position trellis supports the 8,500 grapevines. "This system gives us good fruit exposure, great canopy light penetration, and good control over vigor and structure of the vines," Johnson said. He has planted his vines five feet apart and spaced his rows seven feet apart. He prefers to keep the grape yield low, averaging about three tons to the acre. The entire eight-and-a-half acre vineyard is protected by an electric fence to keep out large animals like deer and bear. It is also necessary to net the entire vineyard to discourage birds from eating the ripe grapes.

"I do love the birds, but I don't want them to eat all of my grapes, and they are still able to get at some of the fruit. This is a prime bird-watching area with dozens of species of birds abounding here," Johnson said. "In fact, I named my vineyard *Colibri* because that means *hummingbird* in many Latin-based languages. We have ten species of hummingbirds that are seen in the Chiricahua Mountains. We feature different hummingbirds on our wine labels."

While waiting three years for the first harvest, expected in 2003, Johnson set about taking wine courses from the University of California at Davis, consulting other vintners, and traveling to Italy to learn the craft of winemaking.

"I tromped around Italy for three weeks with a notebook and a supply of Colibri Vineyard caps," Johnson said. "I was warmly welcomed when I explained I was growing grapes in the desert in Arizona, and when I gave my host a hat from America. I had a great time and learned so much. It was the best education I could have given myself."

When it was time for the first harvest, family and friends gathered to help pick the grapes. Johnson had accumulated the needed equipment for his winery—so the grapes were crushed and de-stemmed by machine; then slowly and gently pushed through a bladder press to remove the juice; put to ferment in small batches in polyvinyl tanks; then aged in oak.

The discarded seeds and stems are used as compost for the vineyard, while some are used to fatten a few pigs. "The pigs love the leftovers, and the resulting meat is tender and sweet," Johnson said. He often treats friends and family to a pig roast after they have helped with the work.

Bob Johnson likes to create complex wines and prefers to make blended wines. "All of our wines are handcrafted at the estate and are unfiltered and unfined, presenting a natural richness and depth," he said. He sells most wines directly from the on-site tasting room and markets some at a few retail locations in Arizona.

Some of his notable and award winning wines include:

Dahiitlhii—for the Navajo word for hummingbird, this is a full-bodied wine blended from Syrah and Petit Verdot grapes. It is a rich purple color with a bouquet of blackberry and black cherry.

Magnificent—vinted from 100 percent estate grown Syrah grapes and then aged for 11 months in French, American and Hungarian oak barrels. It is a full-bodied garnet colored wine with smoke, black cherry and violet bouquet. It won a bronze medal in the 2006 Arizona Governor's choice competition.

Cuvee de Colibri—a wine blended from the estate grown grapes of Mourvedre, Syrah, Grenache Noir, Counoise and Roussanne. It is a layered wine with an earthy nose and sweet spiciness.

Anna's—a blush wine with a bouquet of roses, spice and strawberry, a blend of Grenache, Mourvedre and Counoise. The 2005 vintage was awarded a gold medal in the 2006 Arizona Governor's Choice Awards competition.

Sangre del Sol—a late harvest sweet and spicy white dessert wine, like "liquid sunshine." The 2006 vintage was named the winner of the 2007 Arizona Governor's Choice Award for best dessert wine in Arizona.

Even though the trip to Colibri Vineyards involves traveling several miles on gravel roads, it is well worth the effort. In addition to visiting the vineyard and winery there are other attractions located nearby. The vineyard is close to the famed Chiricahua National Monument. The area is described as one of several "sky island" mountain ranges surrounded by expansive desert grasslands in the southeastern corner of Arizona. The Chiricahua Mountain

Range is an inactive volcanic range twenty miles wide and forty miles long. The Apache Indians described the soaring pinnacles, columns and spires by naming it "The Land of Standing-Up Rocks." The heavily forested canyons within the Monument provide habitat for numerous wildlife, including coatimundi, deer, javalina, and more than 300 species of birds.

About 20 miles south of Colibri Vineyard and Winery is the tiny village of Portal. The American Museum of Natural History Southwestern Research Station, near Portal, serves biologists, geologists, and anthropologists interested in studying the diverse environments and biotas of the Chiricahua Mountains. The station welcomes scientists, volunteers and visitors.

When planning a visit to Colibri Vineyards and Winery it's best to check the web site for driving directions and to call ahead for an appointment. Bob Johnson and family host an open house and wine tasting five times each year, but welcome pre-arranged visitors.

A visit to southeastern Arizona is sure to awaken the senses of any traveler. The journey to Colibri Vineyards evolves from a chalk-dusted road, to a pine-scented canyon, to a wind-carved stone arch. The trip ends at an oasis, where hummingbirds flit from pines to vines. ✾

A SIGN WELCOMES VISITORS TO CHARRON
VINEYARDS IN ARIZONA.

STARLEY TALBOTT

CHARRON VINEYARDS
Vail, Arizona

Leo Cox worked and traveled all over the world before retiring to a small acreage southeast of Tucson, where he planted a vineyard and strived to produce the best "white Merlot wine" in the world.

Cox said as a boy, in the 1930's, he used to help his dad make illegal alcohol in their basement, so it could be sold to feed the family. As a result, Cox grew up disliking alcohol and never drank well into adulthood. "I used to sell my Navy ration of beer for 50 cents a can," he said.

Cox worked in the nuclear power plant industry for years and lived in several foreign countries. His five-year tenure in Spain taught him that enjoying a little wine with a meal could be a good thing. He began exploring the vineyards and wineries in Spain to learn what he could about raising grapes and making wine. "The old world's craftsmanship and dedication to quality sealed my fate. I knew I had to have a vineyard some day." After retiring he tried to buy land in California but found it too expensive and restrictive. Following a ten-year search he located a small acreage south of Vail, Arizona, near his daughter, and moved there in 1994.

Leo and his wife Rhea, along with other family and friends planted 1500 Merlot grapevines. The vineyard was named Charron Vineyards because that is Rhea's maiden name. Leo is a master gardener and thought he'd like to focus on producing just one type of grape, Merlot. He has since added a few Tempranillo vines.

After tirelessly working in the vineyard, installing trellis and drip irrigation lines, Leo assembled the materials needed to make his handcrafted specialty white Merlot wine. The grape harvest is accomplished by hosting a "picking bee," where friends and family come to help pick all the grapes in one day. "It's a ball, we have 40 to 50 people here picking grapes; we have a picnic and lots of old fashioned camaraderie," he said.

The wine is fermented without the skins in poly-vinyl tanks at a cold temperature and allowed to ferment very slowing. "I let it bring out all the good flavors of the grape, making a honeyed crisp wine, similar to Chardonnay, with the medium body of a red wine," Cox said.

Charron Vineyards sells most of its wines at the home tasting room next to the vineyard and Leo attends a few festivals during the year. His first vintage produced 24 cases of wine that he took to a wine tasting in Elgin. "I quickly sold out and was home by 3 p.m., so I was convinced I was on the right track with my wine," he said. He has continued to take extension classes from the University of California, Davis, when possible.

Visitors should make an appointment to visit Charron Vineyards, located on the South Sonoita Highway, 25 miles southeast of Tucson. Check the web site for information.

The 82-year-old winemaker has often been seen on a Tucson television program and was featured in a May 2007, Arizona Highways magazine article. He clearly adores the vineyard and describes his wine as "the elixir of love." ✻

Callaghan Vineyards
Elgin, Arizona

Guarded by purple mountains, woven through golden grass, baked by an orange sun, rooted in red soil, thousands of grapevines stretch toward a blue sky. The Callaghan family planted a vineyard in that southeastern corner of the Arizona desert in 1990.

Harold and Karen Callaghan, along with their son, Kent, planted the original vineyard with Cabernet, Sauvignon, Merlot and Zinfandel vines. "Those rootstocks were suited to the Bordeaux region of France," Kent Callaghan said. "It was one of the hottest summers ever, and we lost a lot of our vines. We quickly changed our strategy and re-planted the vineyard with varieties of Mediterranean or Spanish origin—Tempranillo, Monastrell, Mourvedre and Grenache," he explained. They also added varieties like Syrah, Petite Syrah, Petit Verdot and Riesling.

"The weather is always a concern for our vineyard," Kent said. "After that first hot summer, things improved, and we had our best weather in 2004. In 2005 and 2006 we had some damage from hail, and in 2007 we had too much rain that caused problems with mold and rot."

VINEYARDS IN THE WINTER AT CALLAGHAN VINEYARDS, WITH THE WINERY IN THE BACKGROUND.

No matter the weather and other problems, Kent Callaghan persevered. He took some University of California, Davis, extension wine classes. "I learned a great deal from my own mistakes," he said. Kent eventually turned his grapes into some of the finest wines in the country.

After the grapes from 25,000 vines are harvested, they are allowed to ferment in the half-ton, open-top, picking bins. Kent uses a hot fermenting method and punches down the must (the juice and liquid pulp produced by crushing the grapes) every few days, by hand, using a long-handled tool resembling a giant potato masher. He puts nearly all of the fermented juice, including the white juice, into French oak barrels to finish fermenting. He does not fine or filter any red wines and only a few of the white wines. The white wines age for six to eight months in the barrel; red wines are barrel aged for 10 to 16 months.

Kent's wife, Lisa, serves as the manager of the tasting room at Callaghan Vineyards, between Sonoita and Elgin, Arizona. Kent has crafted dozens of award-winning wines and has honored his wife and two daughters with wines named for them—Lisa's, Claire's and Caitlin's.

Claire's 2004 vintage was served at the White House, on the occasion of the retirement dinner for U.S. Supreme Court Justice, Sandra Day O'Connor, an Arizona native; while Claire's 2005 vintage was named a "great wine" at the 2007 Jefferson Cup competition. The Jefferson Cup Invitational is the only competition that honors the "best of the best" among U.S. wineries from all of America's wine regions. By invitation only, the competing wines must have proven their excellence in competitions and tastings throughout the prior year.

Lisa's 2005 wine was also named a "great wine" at the 2006 Jefferson Cup competition. The wines of Callaghan vineyards have consistently been named outstanding each year from 2003 to the present by the Jefferson Cup judges—including the Syrah, Buena Suerte Cuvee, Zinfandel, Padres, and Cabernet Sauvignon Port.

Callaghan Vineyard's wines were served at the White House during President Bill Clinton's last State Dinner for the Prime Minister of India. They were also served at a White House dinner for the Democratic National Committee.

The production of high-quality wines has always been the primary goal at Callaghan Vineyards. Kent says the vineyard yields are intentionally kept low, two ton per acre, to promote depth of flavor and intensity in the resulting wines. "The red, iron and calcium rich, gravelly clay of the vineyard is one of the most highly-prized soil types for red wine-grapes, wherever it is found in the world," he added.

The vineyard is guarded by an electric fence to keep out deer and other large animals. The tempting grapes have attracted more deer and birds in the last few years, according to Kent Callaghan, who does not net the vines to keep out the birds, but uses alarms to discourage them.

The tasting room is open Friday through Sunday from 11 a.m. to 3 p.m. Beginning in March the winery hosts a "retrospective" tasting each weekend where older bottles of wine are opened to show how the wines age and improve in quality. In November there are new release tasting parties each weekend.

Some of the award-winning wines that may be sampled at Callaghan Vineyards include **Lisa's 2006**—a white wine blended from Viognier, Riesling, Malvasia Bianca, Marsanne and Roussanne grapes, with a bouquet of spiced apple, pear and peach; **Buena Suerte 2006**—a red wine blend of Cabernet Sauvignon, Petit Verdot and Merlot, with a flavor of black fruit, pepper and earth; **Padres 2004**—named for Kent's parents, Harold and Karen, this red wine is a blend of Tempranillo, Cabernet Sauvignon and Merlot, with orange and cherry flavors; **Claire's 2005**—a red wine blended from Mourvedre, Syrah and Petite Sirah grapes, it's like eating cherry/black cherry jelly right out of the jar; and **Caitlin's 2004**—a red wine blended from Petit Verdot, Cabernet Sauvignon and Cabernet Franc grapes, containing hints of herbs, pepper, cinnamon and earth.

In addition to Callaghan Vineyards, travelers can visit several wineries in the immediate vicinity. There are also state parks, hiking and horseback riding, and world class birding sites available. The area's wide-open grasslands are surrounded by a half dozen mountain ranges and flanked by two large ranches: the third generation, family-owned San Ignacio del Babacomari Land Grant and the Empire Ranch. Hollywood has filmed some of the west's most memorable films in the area, including *Oklahoma*, *Red River*, *The Cowboys*, and *The Young Guns*.

Whether tasting wines, the likes of which have been served in the White House, or riding the range like John Wayne, a visit to the grasslands of southeastern Arizona is a pleasing journey. Callaghan Vineyards, in the heart of the Old West and the new wine country, provides a perfect blend of elegance and traditional western charm. ✻

THIS SIGN ANNOUNCING THE ENTRANCE TO
CANELO HILLS WINERY ALSO DEPICTS THE
CANELO HILLS IN THE BACKGROUND.

JOAN MUELLER AND HER DOG AT CANELO HILLS VINEYARD.

CANELO HILLS VINEYARD AND WINERY
Elgin, Arizona

Marriage is a complex partnership. For Tim and Joan Mueller, their partnership evolved to reflect a new love—the marriage of sun-loving grapes to the hot, dry days and cool, clear nights of the high desert.

Joan grows the grapes at Canelo Hills Vineyard, on ten acres in the heart of the Sonoita grasslands. Tim makes the wine at the production facility, next to the vineyard, a few miles between the villages of Sonoita and Elgin, in southeastern Arizona.

The Muellers had dreamed for more than twenty years of someday owning a vineyard and winery. The dream began years before when Tim made dandelion wine during high school and hid it from his parents in a bedroom closet. Joan entered the dream when the two teenagers fell in love and talked of one day living off the land in rural America.

"We postponed our dream during our busy years of careers and raising two children," Joan said. "Whenever we traveled, we visited local wineries and talked with the owners. Tim was also making some darn good wine in our basement," she said.

The pivotal time came during a six-month sabbatical in Arizona's White Mountains in 2001. They fell in love with Arizona and became especially enamored with the historic ranching country of broad grasslands and distant mountains in southeastern Arizona. Some of the peaks there roll down into the *Canelo* Hills, Spanish for cinnamon-colored. They bought ten acres, in the spring of 2004 and planted three acres with Syrah, Mourvedre, Cabernet Sauvignon and Tempranillo grapes.

Tim continues his practice as a psychiatrist as well as being the winemaker. Joan previously worked as a mental health counselor but currently devotes most of her time to managing the vineyard and writing children's stories.

They expanded the vineyard to 3,500 vines by 2008 and added Grenache and Malvasia vines. Joan said there is constant work involved in caring for the vineyard. "After we planted the vines there

TIM MUELLER POURS GRAPES IN THE PRESS AT CANELO HILLS WINERY. (COURTESY OF JOAN MUELLER)

was weed control, planting a cover crop, putting up trellis, training the vines to the trellis, installing and maintaining the drip irrigation system, and pruning the vines," she said.

JOAN MUELLER ENJOYS DRIVING THE TRACTOR TO PERFORM MAINTENANCE WORK AT CANELO HILLS WINERY. (COURTESY OF JOAN MUELLER)

They also had to tear out old, broken-down fencing and install electric fence around the vineyard to keep out deer and other animals. They had just torn out the old fencing and were going to put up the electric fence the next day, when an unwelcome visitor called. "A cow strolled up the driveway and looked at me with her big brown eyes, so I gave her some water, and then she decided to take a walk in the vineyard. I panicked and realized she was going to destroy all our hard work. I couldn't get her to budge, so I had to call on Kent Callaghan, our next-door neighbor and operator of Callaghan Vineyards. He came right over and was able to chase her back towards her home. Needless to say, we were happy to get the electric fence installed the next day," Joan related.

It was a goal of the Muellers to impact the natural environment as little as possible. One method was to plant a cover crop between the vineyard rows to promote soil fertility and vine nutrition. Joan said it's hard to maintain a cover crop in such an arid area, and she didn't want to use precious irrigation water. She chose to plant tepary beans, a legume grown in southern Arizona by the Tohono O'odham Native Americans for centuries. She found the beans grew well and only received moisture from the monsoon rains that fall in the summer months. The mature bean plants are plowed back into the soil to enrich it with nitrogen.

Joan said the monsoon season begins in July when "the morning starts out very clear with blue skies. As the day progresses clouds start popping up over the Huachuca Mountains and gathering into dark thunderheads. The rains come then and are a mixed blessing. Grapevines love the moisture that turns the leaves dark green. On the downside, the damp can start the growth of powdery mildew and the accompanying winds can damage the vines. Sometimes bursts of hail plummet and bruise the grape clusters. In spite of these things, I get a thrill when I see the first clouds appear over the mountains."

Tim said the malfunctioning of machinery seems to be his greatest challenge. He planned to do some work with a tractor one day only to find it wouldn't start because of a dead battery. He said it's pretty isolated at the vineyard so it's not easy to just call a repairman. He had to remove the battery, go to town to get a new one, and then replace it later in the day. "I lost most of a day's work and felt pretty frustrated," he said. "But, in truth, I feel fortunate to be fighting these small battles and not enduring the problems other people in this world have to face," he said.

After three years of hard work getting the vineyard in shape, it was time to harvest the first grapes and begin making wine. The harvest began in August and ended in late September.

Tim wrote about the harvest in an on-line blog on the Canelo Hills web site: "Last week was the end of the active phase of harvest. Coincidently the Harvest Moon occurred on the same night Joan and I pressed the last of the Sangiovese grapes. The moon was a spectacular sight, rising over the Mustang Mountains at dusk and settling behind the Santa Rita Mountains the next morning. As exciting as harvest is for us, it's a totally crazy and busy time. We're picking our grapes and receiving other growers' grapes, crushing the grapes, putting the juice into tanks, punching down the juice a couple times a day, pressing the juice, letting the mixture settle for a day or so, then moving the juice to the barrels that will be their first resting place. The fruit this year looks fabulous, both our own grapes and the grapes that come from other growers in Cochise County."

Tim had made wine from grapes purchased from other growers, so that Canelo Hills Winery would be ready to host visitors at their first annual Wine and Farm Festival in May of 2007. The festival included a farmer's market with alpaca and emu products, goat cheese, baked goods, herbs, jellies and honey, wine, local artwork and publications by local writers.

Canelo Hills Vineyard and Winery hosted a grand opening in September 2007, with tastings of some wines, including **Chardonnay**—a white wine characterized as a honey colored and flavored wine, with a long, lingering finish and balance of tartness and fruitiness; **Riesling**—a crisp, dry white wine with tart acid and a lingering finish; and **Sangiovese**—a light red wine with a brilliant color, a slight oak nose and sharply acid brightness.

Some farming tasks are more favored than others by Joan—she prefers driving a tractor. "One morning I was kind of grumpy with too much work to do, so I decided I needed some tractor-therapy time," she said. "It had rained a little the night before so the conditions were perfect for disking between the rows. Driving the tractor has a bounce and rhythm all of its own. I find it very soothing and it gives me time to think. I started wondering why other women in the wine industry do not do the tractor work, because modern tractors are as easy to drive as cars. Soon I heard a tractor to my right and saw my neighbor bouncing along in his own rhythm; then to my left I saw my other neighbor driving his tractor. There we all were, driving up and down the rows, with the groaning of the engines as background music for our tractor ballet. I thought of it as a very sweet moment where I discovered a secret—men like the powerful feeling they get when on their tractors. I felt privileged to be one of the few women to experience the thrill of the Tractor Ballet."

Whether performing a tractor ballet, pruning vines, picking grapes, pressing juice, bottling wine, sweating in the desert sun, or relaxing in the evening moonlight, the times are satisfying for the Muellers. The vintners of Canelo Hills Vineyard and Winery have found the perfect marriage of vines, wines, and humankind. ✻

THE CANELO HILLS PROVIDE A PLEASING BACKGROUND,
SEEN FROM THE FRONT ENTRANCE TO THE WINERY
AND TASTING ROOM OF SONOITA VINEYARDS.

A SIGN WELCOMES VISITORS TO SONOITA VINEYARDS.

STARLEY TALBOTT

SONOITA VINEYARDS
Elgin, Arizona

Each spring, since 1979, a tradition has been observed at Sonoita Vineyards. The Blessing of the Vineyards Ceremony and Festival, at Arizona's oldest vineyard and winery, provides the inspiration for a productive season.

Ever since the first Blessing, where a "double rainbow appeared amongst dark monsoon clouds," crowds have gathered to witness ministers and priests bless the vines, so that they may grow and prosper during the season, and produce a bountiful crop. The tanks and barrels that play a vital role in transforming the grape juice to wine are also blessed. Following the ceremony there is food, wine tasting, music, dancing and horseback riding.

Back in 1973, when Dr. Gordon Dutt and A. Blake Brophy, established the experimental vineyard—amongst the rolling grassland hills, on a piece of ranchland formerly belonging to the San Ignacio del Babacomari Land Grant—the results of the test were astonishing. Dr. Dutt, a retired soil scientist from the University of Arizona, expected the red grapes to bleach in the intense Arizona sun and produce wines with poor color and low acidity.

"We were surprised to find the results were quite the opposite," Dr. Dutt said. "The red wines showed brilliant color and acidity." He attributed the success to the soil found in the area.

"This part of Arizona is a lot different than most folks imagine, at an altitude of 5,000 feet, set in rolling grasslands, dotted with white oak, the soil is nearly identical to that of Burgundy, France. We've found that our great terra rosa (red clay) soil can produce terrific estate-bottled wines," Dr. Dutt concluded.

Following his experimental success, Dr. Dutt planted 20 acres of vines including the varieties of Chardonnay, Sauvignon Blanc, Cabernet Sauvignon, Merlot, Pinot Noir and Mission grapes. The winery, on a hill overlooking the vineyard, surrounded by scenic mountain ranges, was opened in 1983.

Dr. Dutt is the owner of Sonoita Vineyards and served as the chief vineyard manager and winemaker for many years. He continues as the vineyard manager, but has employed other staff to tend to the winemaking and management of the tasting room.

A serendipity experience brought the current winemaker, Fran Lightly, to the Sonoita/Elgin area, where the vast grasslands are dotted with vineyards, cattle, deer, antelope and horses. Fran and his wife, Kathy, had spent three weeks, in 2006, visiting wineries in Texas, New Mexico and Arizona, looking for a place to re-locate from their California home.

"Sonoita Vineyard was the last stop on our tour, and we loved the beauty of the area," Fran said. Dr. Dutt was at the tasting room when Fran and Kathy arrived, was pleased to give them a tour, and accepted the calling card Fran left behind.

"Dr. Dutt phoned me shortly after we arrived back in California, and offered me the job as winemaker. Two months later I reported for work, in May of 2006," Fran said. His nine years of experience as a winemaker in Livermore, California, was an asset he brought with him to Sonoita Vineyards.

Lightly had grown up in Minnesota, where he owned a deli and catering business, moved to Phoenix in 1990, and then to California, where he became interested in viticulture. He already possessed a degree in chemistry, so he enrolled at California State University at Fresno, where he studied enology.

Bringing his diverse experience along, Lightly found the transition to producing wine from Arizona grapes to be "quite easy." He says the climate and soil are ideal and the weather is "fantastic." "It's very rare for the temperature in our area to hit a hundred degrees in the summer and the evenings are cool. We have a 30 to 35 degree difference in temperature ranges from day to night. The location of the vineyard on a hillside means that the cold air drains downward and we seldom have freeze problems."

The vineyard is watered with a drip irrigation system, and the entire acreage is fenced with a seven and a half foot high fence, to keep out deer and antelope. Some fertilizer is applied to the vineyard through the drip irrigation system. Sonoita Vineyards also buys grapes from other Arizona grape growers to produce their award winning wines.

State of-the-art equipment is found in the production area of the winery. The wines are fermented both in polyvinyl and stainless steel tanks. After the grapes are de-stemmed and crushed by machine, the juice is pressed through a new three-ton capacity membrane press. All of the red wines are aged in American or Hungarian oak barrels. All wines are bottled by a semi-automatic bottling machine and hand labeled. Most of the wine labels include pictures created by local artists that feature regional scenery.

In addition to his winemaking duties, Fran Lightly, assists in the management of the tasting room. "I think it is crucial to be open for visitors, so we keep the tasting room open seven days a week from 10 a.m. to 4 p.m.," he said. Ninety percent of the 3,500 cases of Sonoita Vineyard wines are sold from the tasting room.

Visitors come from all over the world to try the wines at Sonoita and other nearby wineries. The area currently has seven wineries and more are popping up all the time. In addition to wineries, guests can experience the highlights of the Sonoita, Elgin and Patagonia area including hiking, horseback riding, world-class birding, several state parks, museums and ghost towns.

The nearby Arizona Horseback Experience offers a 3-hour trail ride that concludes with a visit to Sonoita Vineyards, where participants can taste several wines including **Cochise County Colombard**—a fresh and fruity white wine with a flowery bouquet and refreshing finish; **Arizona Sunset**—a semi-sweet fruity rose wine; **Angel Wings**—a white wine derived from Mission grapes, with a delicate aroma of nectarines and apples; **Sonoita Pinot Noir**—a red wine with black cherry and raspberry flavors, a consistent medal winner on both the East and West Coast; and **Arizona Cabernet Sauvignon**—a full-bodied red wine with outstanding character, it has won numerous awards and been praised by national wine judges. A vintage of Cabernet Sauvignon was served at the 1989 Presidential Inauguration of George Bush.

The **Angel Wings** wine holds special significance because a Lutheran minister, who asked for a light wine to be used for communion, first requested it. Members of the congregation then wanted to buy the wine. In turn, the wine became popular at a Catholic church and is now served for communion at six area churches.

FRAN LIGHTLY, WINEMAKER AT SONOITA VINEYARDS,
POURS A TASTE OF WINE FROM A BARREL AT THE WINERY.

In addition to the spring Blessing Festival, Sonoita Vineyards also hosts two other annual events—an Augustfest, a two-day celebration of the harvest; and a St. Martin's New Release Festival in November. The facility also has space for special events including weddings, anniversary parties, business meetings, private gatherings and luncheon tours.

Spectacular views from the veranda or balcony of the winery provide visitors a scenic panorama of rolling mile-high grasslands, punctuated by oak glades and yucca patches. In the distance are the Huachuca, Whetstone, Santa Rita and Mustang Mountains. Nearby are the oak-forested Canelo Hills stretching southward to the Arizona-Mexico border. Sonoita Vineyards is truly blessed with nature's benevolence. ❋

ALCANTARA VINEYARDS
Cottonwood, Arizona

Eagles soar, like giant magic carpets, above the cliffs bordering Alcantara Vineyards. At the confluence of the Verde River and Oak Creek—where shepherds used to ford the water with their flocks of sheep—a new winery brings enchantment to the landscape.

Barbara Predmore, owner and proprietor, described this oasis in the Arizona desert as "a dream venture created when she reached mid-life." Barbara and her husband, Bob, established the vineyard to provide their family and partners "the opportunity to live the dream of working and developing a vineyard community and winery, making wines that are comparable to the best of California and Europe," she said.

Barbara Predmore's dream began years earlier, as a member of the family that operated Martin-Weyrich Vineyards in Paso Robles, California. She realized at a young age that the lifestyle created by living near a vineyard was desirable. She went on to marry, follow a different career, raise children, and finally return to her roots.

THE WINERY AND TASTING ROOM OF
ALCANTARA WINERY IN ARIZONA.

The new vineyard in Arizona was named for Barbara's grandmother, whose maiden name was Dolores Alcantara, the daughter of a Philippine governor. "She taught me that family, faith and the land are very important aspects of life. She taught me to respect the people who worked the land. And, she taught me that you always share what you have and give back to the land and the people."

Barbara's grandmother also told her that the name *Alcantara*, in Spanish, meant either a bridge or water well. "Either way, both meanings describe what I want Alcantara to be—a bridge bringing people together or a water well that provides life," Barbara said.

Those principles govern the way Barbara operates Alcantara Vineyard. She considers herself a farmer, and manages the land as organically as possible. Barbara said the dry Arizona climate is ideal for grapes, because they have deep root systems, requiring only a small amount of water, and there are very few problems with disease or pests.

The vineyard was planted with Merlot and Syrah grapes, in 2004, on a portion of the 87-acre land-site. By 2008, there were 12,000 vines marching down the gently sloping shelves of limestone and rocky soil toward the horseshoe curve of the Verde River. No water from the river is used, however, and the vines are watered from a well utilizing a drip irrigation system. Barbara added more vines each year, with a number of different varieties, including Merlot, Syrah, Petite Syrah, Cabernet Sauvignon, Zinfandel, Mourvedre, Charbono, and Pinot Noir. When the vines begin to form grape clusters, Barbara prefers to "drop" or cut off some of the clusters so the vines produce a small, but better quality crop. The first harvest, in August of 2007, produced six ton of grapes from the original planting of Merlot and Syrah grapes. All of the grapes are handpicked at harvest.

The winery was begun on a modest scale, as well. The equipment includes a small crusher, bladder press, a few tanks, and a few oak barrels. Barbara has employed a neighboring winemaker, for the present time, to help make the wine for Alcantara.

The atmosphere at the Alcantara tasting room is meant to be personable and inviting for guests. Leather couches are grouped around tables filled with magazines in front of a cozy fireplace.

The small tasting room will someday be enlarged, as will the entire complex. Future plans involve the addition of a café bistro, information center and a bed and breakfast inn. Barbara imagines visitors touring the vineyard and winery, listening to music, and perhaps attending a special event at the winery. She also envisions the numerous vineyards of the Verde Valley being recognized as a unique American Vineyard Appellation in the future.

Barbara hopes to encourage people to visit the area and become "one with the land." She'd also like people to consider growing small vineyards all around the area—she says it only takes a small acreage to grow a few grapes. "It's so satisfying, they don't have to operate a winery, I'll buy the grapes they grow," she said.

Alcantara Vineyards is located in the center of a tourist triangle, leading to Arizona's north country from Phoenix. Tourist opportunities abound in the nearby towns of Cottonwood, Jerome, Sedona, Flagstaff and the Grand Canyon. Cottonwood has many outdoor activities available including a ride on the Verde Canyon Railroad, or a visit to Tuzigoot National Monument, an old Native American dwelling. Jerome is a historic mining town where the entire town is on the National Register of Historic Places. Flagstaff is the gateway to the Grand Canyon. Sedona is renowned for its scenic red buttes, monoliths, and surrounding forests—and is a center for traditional and contemporary arts.

Sedona Adventure Outfitters and Guides offer a guided float trip down the Verde River that ends with a wine tasting at Alcantara Vineyards. Visitors can taste wines from bottles with Arizona scenes on the label, created by local artists. The wines include **Chardonnay**—a 100 percent Arizona white wine with a flavor of green apple and pear; **Viognier**—a rich white wine with aromas of peaches, apricots and honeysuckle; **Syrah**—a bold and dark ruby Australian-style red wine, aged in American oak; **Merlot**—a deep ruby red wine, aged for 14 months in French and American oak; and **Petite Syrah**—a dark red wine, with ripe cherry, red plum and a hint of coconut flavor.

Barbara Predmore and her German Shepherd dogs welcome guests to the tasting room. In addition to tending the vineyard and winery, Barbara is raising old style German Shepherds. "We are attempting to bring back the original breed, which are larger than

BARBARA PREDMORE GIVES HER GERMAN SHEPHERD PUPPY A HUG AT HER WINERY IN ARIZONA.

American Shepherds and have a very docile temperament. They are family oriented and are not aggressive, unless the family is in danger. They watch over the vineyard and keep unwanted critters away," she said.

At the convergence of Oak Creek and the Verde River, there is a very spiritual connection where two bodies of water come together—and where people come together to celebrate life—at Alcantara Vineyards. "I love the tasting room and the people that come there. When I talk to people and hear their stories, it reinforces my belief in what I'm doing," Barbara said. ✹

Jerome Winery

Jerome, Arizona

Copper, gold and silver brought explorers to Jerome, Arizona, in the late nineteenth century. Art, history, shopping, food and wine bring people there today.

John McLoughlin opened Jerome Winery near the top of a steep hillside overlooking historic buildings and the huge open-pit, abandoned, copper mine below. Visitors come from all over the world to explore the historic mining town, situated two hours northwest of Phoenix, and less than an hour southwest of Sedona.

John's sparkling blue eyes twinkle with pleasure when he tells winery guests tales from Jerome's past and relates the story of how he became a vintner. At the age of 16, John spent a year as an exchange student in Germany. "As luck would have it, my German family was composed of great wine enthusiasts. I learned to appreciate wine the European way—leisurely enjoyed with excellent food and good

JOHN MCLAUGHLIN, OWNER AND WINEMAKER, POURS WINE AT HIS JEROME WINERY IN JEROME, ARIZONA.

conversation. I experienced many good German, French and Italian wines and learned that wine should be imbibed for enjoyment, not to get drunk."

Years later, back in the United States, John traveled to numerous California wineries, spending weeks at a time working in different facilities, and learning the craft of wine making from California experts. He also traveled to many other countries around the world, visiting wineries, and learning from master winemakers.

In 2000, John purchased property south of Willcox, Arizona. The land was located 18 miles down Kansas Settlement Road, in country that had once been roamed by the Apache Indian chiefs, Geronimo and Cochise.

John began to prepare several acres on the new property for planting grapes. His mother, Marge Black-Graziano, and his older sister, Melanie, also helped out. John's greatest admirer is his mother—she said her son has been "playing in the dirt since he was two years old, and his love of growing things has continued to develop over the years." Family, friends and a small crew of workers gathered in 2004, under the shadow of the Dragoon, Chiricahuas, and the Dos Cabezas Mountains, in southeastern Arizona, to "play in the dirt" and turn the Willcox land from a "big field of weeds to a big field of dreams," at the newly created Dragoon Vineyards.

"We laid the pipe that would bring water to the vineyard, in the freshly dug trenches. We pounded in the stakes, hung the water lines, stretched the wire for the vines to climb, dug the holes, mucked out the mud, gently placed the bare root vines in the holes, kindly covered the roots with mud, and moved along row by row, creating a vineyard," Marge Graziano said. "Daybreak to dusk, for weeks on end we planted. Sore backs, bruised knees, dirty fingernails and dusty bodies gave way to pure pleasure, as green leaves pushed forth from thin brown trunks. Weeks later, tiny tendrils wound along the trellis wires and small clusters of grapes portended the future and a healthy crop," she extolled.

It would take four years of weeding, pruning and training the 45 varieties of vines to produce the first grape crop, expected to be harvested in the fall of 2008. The vines are nourished by a drip watering system fed by several wells and pumped into tanks for storage. Many of the grapevines are experimental varieties and John says it remains to be seen how well they will grow and produce. As the vines were maturing, John was often making the six-hour drive from the vineyard to the winery in Jerome.

John produced all the first wines sold at the Jerome Winery in a facility in California, from California-grown grapes. He expects to soon produce all his wines from Arizona estate grown grapes. Future plans include establishing a wine production facility at the Willcox location, along with another tasting room. The family also plans to host wine tours and educational seminars at the Willcox vineyard, in addition to keeping the winery open in Jerome.

It was Marge's dream that brought the family to Jerome and led to the founding of Jerome Winery. Marge had moved to Arizona as a young adult and established herself selling insurance in the Phoenix area. She loved driving up through the mountains and visiting in the quaint old mining town of Jerome.

The town had been built on Cleopatra Hill above a vast deposit of copper, where miners staked the first claims in 1876. Jerome grew rapidly from a tent city to a prosperous company town that produced billions of dollars of copper from its underground and pit mines. The hills rattled, buildings cracked, and the ground shifted when miners opened pits with dynamite. Today's visitors can still see the sliding jail that moved 225 feet down a hillside and rests across the road from its original site. Eventually the mines were closed, due to a number of factors, including copper prices, labor problems, depressions and wars. The population dwindled from a peak of 15,000, to around 50 people, by the late 1950's. Jerome became the home of people in the "counter culture" during the 1960's and 1970's. It also evolved into a haven for artists, who renovated homes and opened abandoned shops. Today it thrives with writers, artists, musicians, shopkeepers, chefs, historians and families, who make the community a colorful town, built on a rich foundation of history and lore.

Adding to the 450 residents that are building today's tourist town of Jerome are Marge Black-Graziano and her children. On a visit several years ago, Marge was gazing out the window of one of the art galleries perched on the mountainside. "I saw an old house, down the hillside, and across from the old copper mine. I had a strange feeling

MARGE BLACK GRAZIANO POURS WINE FOR VISITORS, REBECCA WESTRATE OF FERNDALE, MICHIGAN, AND DAWNE BELL AND BOB VANDER VOORD OF ALBUQUERQUE, NEW MEXICO, AT JEROME WINERY.

about the house and asked the gallery owner about it," she said. The gallery owner told her it was called the "Honeymoon Cottage" and was owned by a man who lived in Costa Rica. Marge contacted the man, who didn't want to sell the house, but she told him, "you must sell me the house, you'll never love it like I will."

Marge was able to buy the house and began to restore it to its former glory. In 1921, Jimmy Douglas, the owner of the Little Daisy Mine, gave his son Lewis a wedding gift, the little cottage overlooking the Verde Valley, which came to be known as the "Honeymoon Cottage." Lewis and his bride, Peggy, lived in the house for only one year, because Jerome was a rough and tumble town, and Peggy, it was said, longed for another life back East. The cottage had many owners and finally fell into disrepair. The restoration of the home including new wiring, plumbing, refinishing the original wood floors, new windows and doors, and fresh paint was finished in time for the wedding of Marge's second daughter, Carrie, in April 2003.

Marge travels back and forth from her home in Mesa, nearly every weekend, to enjoy her second home at the Honeymoon Cottage, and help out at the winery. "The winery is in a perfect location on Clark Street, in the renovated old nurse's quarters, near the center of town," she said. "The world comes to see us in Jerome. I get a chance to tell stories from Jerome's past, and I get a chance to be on stage, fulfilling an old dream I had of being a dancer and entertainer."

The family, including Marge, John, Melanie, and Melanie's husband, Isaiah, love to entertain guests at the winery and tell them stories—like how there are two ghosts who sometimes make appearances at the winery. According to John, one ghost is called Justy, because he appears to be an old miner; and the other ghost is called Madam, because she appears to be a woman, who might possibly have been a Madam, during the rough and rowdy mining days.

Ghosts or not, visitors make their way to the hilltop winery in droves. They can enjoy a variety of wines, which are often served with a fruit and cheese plate, in the cozy tasting room, or enjoy the view from the outside patio. Wines ranging from Chenin Blanc, to Chardonnay, to Merlot, to Syrah, to Almond or Raspberry, are served from bottles adorned with old family photos. John estimates that a million and a half visitors come through the facility every year, which is open 365 days a year.

The proprietors of Jerome Winery hope to leave a lasting legacy— as prominent as the one left by hardy pioneers from an earlier era. As Marge Black-Graziano says, "It's so cool to serve wine that is a product that your child has made. It makes me so proud." ❧

FORMER RANCH BUILDINGS WERE CONVERTED TO THE
PAGE SPRINGS WINERY AT PAGE SPRINGS, ARIZONA.

GEESE ASSIST IN THE MANAGEMENT OF
PAGE SPRINGS VINEYARD.

Page Springs Vineyards and Cellars
Cornville, Arizona

The diversity of Arizona, from its saguaro-studded deserts to rugged volcanic peaks, captured the heart and imagination of a young man from New England when he traveled west. One day, that journey ended at a vineyard and winery in northern Arizona.

Amongst his treks in the American West, Eric Glomski hiked in the Grand Canyon of Arizona, and knew he'd found the place he wanted to spend the rest of his life. "The Arizona Mountains just go on forever during sunset, layer after layer of purple mountain majesty, with open space, room to breathe, and endless views," he said.

Eric enrolled at Prescott College, where he studied ecology, and formed a river restoration company after graduating. For the next two years he hiked hundreds of miles through the Prescott National Forest, assessing the condition of the waterways there. Many old, abandoned homesteads, where apple orchards still grew, caught his attention during those hikes. "I filled my backpack with apples and brought them home to make cider," he said.

After meeting a local winemaker, Eric decided to turn a batch of apples into wine. Several months later, "just as spring was awakening our high desert landscape, I was invited to a party to celebrate the vernal equinox. I opened the first bottle of apple wine and was stunned. I sat there sniffing the wine and swishing it around in my mouth. The apples were there, the texture, the tartness, and the wonderful sweet perfume. But there was more, the trees themselves, the smell of decaying leaves, the fall flowers growing amongst the dried grasses, the wind in the trees, the tiny, riddling stream, and even the old rock foundations of the houses of the people who planted those trees, and who once played and labored in that field. The wine was that place in a bottle—liquid landscape."

That experience proved to be an epiphany for Eric Glomski. He bought books on making wine, spent time tasting wine, and eventually ended up working in the vineyards of California, so that he could learn the craft of winemaking from start to finish.

When Eric landed a job as a harvest worker at the David Bruce Winery in California, he didn't know how long he would stay there, but he knew his ultimate goal was to make world-class wine in the central Arizona highlands. As he worked his way up the ladder, he never lost sight of the dream to own land in Arizona.

"I lived in the back of my pickup truck and worked eighteen-hour days during the harvest at David Bruce Winery. I can still remember the first time I walked into the cellar there. The smell of fermenting wine, the barrels, the big, shiny, stainless steel tanks were magical. The 1997 harvest was larger than expected. We had so much fruit we were fermenting grapes in the parking lot. I would put on hip waders and jump into the fermenting tanks to punch down the grapes during the night, gazing up at the stars while music blasted on the stereo," Eric related.

The young Glomski stayed at DBW for five years, working his way from harvester, to assistant production manager, production manager, assistant winemaker and finally to co-winemaker. He says he learned so much there and was greatly influenced by Ken Foster, who trained him to understand how technology affects the quality of wine. "He also showed me how blending is one of the true arts of winemaking."

"I was lucky enough to oversee the production of one of the largest blends at DBW, the Central Coast Pinot Noir. To achieve that blend, I worked with a number of vineyards throughout the Central Coast," Eric said. "It was an exciting time for me and the wine industry."

During his California tenure, Eric also learned that "great wines are made in the vineyard, not the winery." It was this philosophy that guided him when he established his family vineyard and winery in Arizona and created a mission statement:

"It is our goal to create delicious wines that express the unique character of our landscape. We believe that to make great wine, we must take just as much responsibility for the lands we steward as the community we live in. We feel strongly that growing grapes, making wine and raising a glass is a cultural ritual that fosters friendship, brings together families, and unites communities."

Before that mission statement could be created, though, Eric had to find his way back to Arizona. He met some growers from Arizona during a grape symposium in Sacramento, in 2002, and expressed his desire to return to Arizona. The following year Eric became the winemaker for Echo Canyon Winery in Sedona, Arizona, where he worked for a year.

Finally, in 2004, Eric and his family were able to purchase a piece of property, along the banks of Oak Creek, in Page Springs, just south of Sedona. His dream began to become reality and Eric described the land as "one of the most beautiful places on earth."

The name for the venture was a natural, because the bountiful flow of nearby Page Springs nourishes the vineyard. The springs were named for James Page, who had settled the area in the late 1800's, where he grew and hauled vegetables by ox team to the nearby mining town of Jerome. Page also established the Page Springs Fish Hatchery, in 1928, which was acquired by the State of Arizona in 1945.

The land the Glomski family purchased also included the buildings of the original working ranch. The old barn was turned into the winery and tasting room, and the bunkhouse became the office and conference room. Rocks were cleared from the fields before the grapevines were planted. The rocks were then used to form terraces and the borders and arches of a pathway leading from the winery to the vineyard and Oak Creek.

"Nestled along the banks of Oak Creek and on the lower flanks of House Mountain volcano, this land is truly unique," Eric said. "The sandy, clay-loam soil overlays a layer of volcanic rock that includes limestone-like sediments. The sub soils are alkaline, much like the limestone of the southern Rhone region of France. These soils contribute character to our grapes and the alkalinity tempers the vigor of our aggressive Rhone varieties," he explained.

The vineyard was planted with Syrah, Mourvedre, Grenache, Petite Syrah, Cabernet Pfeffer, Rousanne, Viognier, Marsanne and Petite Verdot grape varieties. The climate in the area is considered to be much like the climate of the Mediterranean. "The bulk of our rain comes in the winter. Summers are generally hot and dry. In the summer we have up to a 40 degree fluctuation

from day to night, which is critical for the development of flavors and other grape components that are critical to making fine wine," Eric added.

As the business grew, Page Springs Cellars employed several people to assist with the management of the vineyard and winery. Craig Martinsen, vineyard manager, says that Page Springs is committed to farming without the use of chemicals. Management practices include the use of animal fertilizer and the planting of a natural cover crop, including wildflowers, clovers and legumes, between the grapevine rows. The rows are five feet apart; with the vines spaced every five feet and trained to climb on a Vertical Shoot Position trellis system. The vineyard is watered using precision drip and micro-sprinkler irrigation. Geese and ducks roam among the vines to dispose of insects and weeds.

A challenge in recent years has been managing cold air that damaged and killed some of the vines in the lower portion of the vineyard. Thus, a fan was installed to remove cold air from the vineyard floor. "The fan acts like a vacuum, sucking the cold air off the ground and channeling it up, like in a chimney, to remove it from the area," Martinsen, said.

Martinsen explained that the team at Page Springs has developed a management program, called "Hand-Made Vine to Wine Program," to assist other small growers in the area. They have successfully installed about 20 small-acreage vineyards throughout the Verde Valley. Landowners who wish to participate will receive installation, management, harvesting and winemaking services from Page Springs Cellars. "It's a great way to add value to a small acreage and increase the appreciation for viticulture in the area. These growers don't have to quit another job, but can still enjoy the pleasure of producing their own grapes and wine," he said.

Investors from Page Springs Cellars purchased additional property, formerly the Dos Cabezas Vineyard at Willcox, Arizona, in 2007. It was well established, having been planted in 1983 with Rhone and Spanish varietal grapes. The vineyard was renamed as Cochise Stronghold in honor of the Apache leader, Cochise, who once roamed the bordering Dragoon Mountains in southeastern Arizona.

Eric Glomski, chief winemaker at Page Springs Cellars, now has a wide range of grape varieties with which to create great wines. This helps to fulfill another goal expressed in his mission statement—"good wine is not strictly the esoteric fare of nobility. Wine is for the people. We have set out to share our passion and interest in wine with everyone from the first time sipper to the seasoned enthusiast."

The winery at Page Springs Cellars is filled to the brim with the usual equipment necessary for producing wine—a mechanical crusher and de-stemmer, bladder press, stainless steel tanks, plastic vats, and French and Hungarian oak barrels. Wines that are bottled there include **Vino del Barrio Blanca**—a crisp and fruity white wine, translating to mean the "neighborhood wine;" **Enz Mourvedre**—

a red wine with flavors of white pepper and roses; **ECIPS**—a spicy red wine blended from Syrah, Mourvedre, Grenache, Carignon, and Cabernet Pfeffer grapes, named by spelling Spice backwards; **Mules Mistake**—a bright and fruity wine that came about because a worker made a mistake in the blending of the juices, that turned out so well, it continues to be produced. **El Serrano** is the signature wine of Page Springs Cellars, a deep, rich red wine from a blend of Mourvedre, Syrah and Cabernet Pfeffer grapes.

Visitors to Page Springs Cellars will find that "wine is within everyone's reach," forming a bond between land, grapes, wine, friends, and family. Guests may experience this liquid landscape—the one that fulfilled the dream of a young man who fell in love with Arizona and wine. ✺

UTAH

Blue mountain vistas can be seen from the vineyards at Spanish Valley Vineyards near Moab, Utah.

Spectacular rock formations form the background to Spanish Valley Vineyards south of Moab, Utah.

STARLEY TALBOTT

Spanish Valley Vineyards and Winery
Moab, Utah

Towering red rock cliffs dominate the desert valley, while distant blue mountain vistas hover over a portion of Utah landscape called Spanish Valley. South of the town of Moab, at Spanish Valley Vineyards, grapevines with verdant leaves and juicy berries, creep up to meet the dry, sunlit, fall sky that promises to ripen the grapes to perfection.

Stacy and Cory Dezelsky, owners of Spanish Valley Vineyards, prepared to harvest a bumper crop of grapes in 2007—in their eighth year of ownership. They had spent a decade longer taking care of the vineyard for previous owners, then buying the property and coaxing the vineyards back to full production. Stacy said the five acres had been planted with grapes more than 30 years earlier but had been allowed to malinger for years.

"Our area, at an elevation of 4,800 feet, dry climate with long, sunny days and cool nights is ideal for growing grapes," Stacy said. "Our soil, consisting of a top layer of sandy clay, followed by a second layer of clay, and a third layer of rock and sand, helps the soil to retain moisture. The vines also pull certain ingredients from the soil that make the grapes and wine produced from them display unique flavors. We don't have to make many adjustments to our wine, we just let the natural flavors come through. We're just farmers at heart and we make pretty straightforward wines," Stacy concluded.

Even though Cory and Stacy are both farmers at heart, it was a long journey that led them to a vineyard in Spanish Valley, Utah. Cory had grown up on a farm near Orem, Utah, and Stacy had grown up in Illinois.

Stacy moved to Salt Lake City, Utah, in 1979, after graduating from the University of Illinois with a degree in Parks and Recreation Administration. She worked as a snow cat operator at Snow Bird Ski Resort for several seasons. Some of her co-workers were from New Zealand, so at the end of ski season, she followed them to New Zealand. She worked in vineyards near Hawkes Bay, on the North Island, learning to prune vines. When she returned to the United States, Stacy worked in vineyards in the Napa Valley of California. She eventually returned to Utah, where she worked as a whitewater raft guide on the Colorado River, near Moab. She met Cory there, in 1987, where he

STACY AND CORY DEZELSKY EXPLAIN HOW WINE IS PRODUCED IN THEIR SPANISH VALLEY VINEYARDS WINERY NEAR MOAB, UTAH.

was managing a restaurant. Stacy and Cory bought the property south of Moab, and both worked at area restaurants at night while working on the farmland during the day.

The couple nursed the old vines back to life and planted new vines, ending up with 4,000 vines of Gewurztraminer, Riesling, Cabernet Sauvignon and Syrah. They use a three-wire trellis system to support the vines and water the vineyard using drip irrigation. They don't net for birds, but use noisemakers to discourage the birds, starlings being the worst offenders. They also plant roses at the ends of the vine rows. "Roses are very sensitive to pests and disease. They alert us to potential problems in the vineyard before the vines are affected," Stacy said.

They sold their first grape crops to a nearby winery and to wineries in western Colorado. When Colorado producers began growing more grapes, the Dezelskys lost their market, so they decided to open their own winery in 1999.

"Utah has very restrictive laws concerning liquor," Stacy said. "It's been a real challenge selling wine in Utah," Stacy said. But, by banding together, the Utah vintners were able to convince the state legislature to change the laws and allow commercial wineries in Utah. "There is still room for improvement, as we cannot ship our wine either out-of-state or in-state," Stacy added.

They still sell some of their mature grapes to other wineries. The family, including 11-year-old son, Troy, harvest the grapes, along with the help of local Navajo women, who "do a good job of picking grapes," Stacy said. Most of the harvest is completed from mid-

August to Labor Day weekend. About one to one-and-a-half ton of Riesling grapes are picked for a late harvest, sweet wine. They also make some wine from locally grown cherries.

The winery produced 1,000 gallons of wine in 1999 and grew to around 2,400 gallons in 2007. The Dezelskys use both polyvinyl and stainless steel tanks for fermentation and use oak chips in aging some of their wines. The wine is bottled and labeled by hand with labels designed by Stacy.

Spanish Valley Vineyards wine was awarded a silver medal in the New World International Wine Competition for their 2002 Cabernet Sauvignon. They were also featured on the 2004 cover of "Wine Spectator" magazine. Some of their most popular wines include **Chenin Blanc**—a very dry wine with a touch of oak; **Gewürztraminer**—an off dry wine with citrus flavors; **Riesling**—a crisp, fruity, apple flavored wine; **Cherry Wine**—a wine with flavors of tart cherry pie; **Zinfandel**—a light bodied and slightly sweet wine; **Syrah**—a dry wine with black pepper flavors; **Cabernet Sauvignon**—a dry wine with berry flavors; and **Late Harvest Riesling**—a sweet, fruity dessert wine.

Stacy believes that wine touring in America is a major industry and should be promoted locally along with the natural wonders, music, films and art. "The potential for growth in the area as a low-impact tourist industry is very important," she said.

There is a wealth of outdoor beauty and recreational opportunities in the Moab area. Visitors can enjoy hiking, biking, jeep tours and Colorado River rafting. Red rock canyons abound including Arches National Park, Canyonlands National Park and Dead Horse Point State Park. The area is generally considered a "sports paradise." Visitors may find it a surprise to find three fine wineries in the area, including Spanish Valley Vineyards, Castle Creek Winery and Round Mountain Vineyards and Winery.

"Winemaking is a very personal business," Stacy concluded. "People are emotionally involved. I believe they like to see the vines growing, like to see what harvest is like, and like to see the winemaking process. We try to provide that experience at Spanish Valley Vineyards," she said.

Utah's wineries are a fledgling business that is beginning to make its mark in the world of wine. Stacy Dezelsky hopes it will no longer be "Utah's best-kept secret." ❧

THE VINEYARDS AT CASTLE CREEK WINERY ARE ACCENTED BY SOARING RED CLIFFS AND WIDE BLUE SKIES ALONG THE COLORADO RIVER IN UTAH.

WILL FRYER DISPLAYS THE LARGE STAINLESS STEEL TANKS USED TO FERMENT WINE AT CASTLE CREEK WINERY NEAR MOAB, UTAH.

CASTLE CREEK WINERY
Moab, Utah

If you've ever seen a western cowboy movie, chances are you've seen the majestic rock canyons where the Red Cliffs Ranch is located, along the Colorado River, in eastern Utah. Red Cliffs Ranch and Lodge is also home to Castle Creek Winery.

John Wayne and Maureen O'Hara starred in the movie *Rio Grande*, filmed at Red Cliffs Ranch in 1948. *Wagon Master* followed in 1949 and dozens of movies and commercials were filmed there over the years. Those many Hollywood stars, including John Wayne, Henry Fonda, Lee Marvin, Billy Crystal, Geena Davis, Susan Sarandon and Robert Duvall would have had a hard time enjoying a glass of wine at Red Cliffs Lodge in those days, however. For years it was illegal to make or sell wine commercially in Utah.

That all changed in 1988 when local grape growers formed a loose-knit organization and successfully lobbied the Utah legislature to legalize wineries. Up to that time, growers in the area were forced to sell their grapes to nearby wineries, mainly in the Grand Junction, Colorado, area.

One of the early wineries in Moab, Utah, was Arches Winery, which operated from 1989 to 1998 in Moab. Arches Winery was then sold to Colin and Will Fryer, and moved to Red Cliffs Ranch, 15 miles northeast of Moab. The name was changed to Castle Creek Winery. Will Fryer said the story of vineyards and wineries in Utah began nearly thirty years prior to the time Castle Creek Winery was opened.

"In the 1970's the Four Corners Regional Economic Development Commission did some test plantings of wine grapes in the Moab area. Hot days, cool nights and sandy soil produced wine grapes of unique, exceptional quality. The late summer sun encourages good sugar content with high acid levels necessary to produce well-balanced high-quality wine," he said. Will went on to explain that eastern Utah is in many ways similar to the eastern Mediterranean, where the wild grapes that became classic European wine grape varieties originated.

Since the test plot results were positive, several farmers planted vineyards, in the early 1980's, with the help and encouragement of the Utah Agricultural Department. When the first crops were harvested a few years later, however, there was no local market to sell the grapes. "In fact, the new growers discovered it was illegal to make or sell wine in Utah. One department of the government had encouraged farmers to grow wine grapes but another department said no to using the grapes for their intended purpose," Fryer said.

Even though the right to make and sell wine was granted in 1988, the state imposed rules and heavy taxes making it difficult to make a profit. In 2004, additional legislation made it possible for wineries to be open during busy tourist seasons and the taxes were reduced to a reasonable level.

Castle Creek Winery produces around 14,000 gallons of red and white wine made from grapes purchased from other growers. They planted several acres of grapes in 2005 and hope to eventually produce wines from mostly estate and locally grown grapes.

Will Fryer had never intended to be a winemaker. In fact, he was a carpenter, when his Dad, Colin, bought the winery. "I was appointed to take over as the winemaker, so I got a crash course from the University of California, Davis, attended a number of seminars, and did a lot of reading," he said.

With the help of Charleen and Ray Radley and a few other workers, Castle Creek Winery has produced several award-winning wines. Charleen is officially the tasting room manager but wears many other hats as well.

"I love to work with the grapes. I enjoyed planting the grapes, and I like to help with pruning. I like crushing the berries and helping out in the winery where needed," Charleen said. Her husband, Ray, is the all-around-man in the winery and is expert in bottling and hand labeling each bottle of wine.

When Charleen pours wine in the western-style tasting room, with knotty pine walls and Mexican tiled floors, she also guides visitors through the grape growing and wine making process by presenting the following seminar:

"Wine grapes are harvested in the late summer. White wine grapes are separated from their stems and leaves and then squeezed

CHARLEEN RADLEY DISPENSES WINE AND KNOWLEDGE
TO VISITORS AT CASTLE CREEK WINERY.

in a big metal crusher that separates the juice from the skins and seeds of the grape. The juice is then pumped into refrigerated tanks and yeast is added to the juice to start fermentation. White wine is fermented at low temperatures at a slow rate to bring out the fruit flavors of the grape."

"Red wine grapes are crushed but not separated from the skins and seeds as white wine grapes are. Instead, the must of juice, skins and seeds is pumped into vats where yeast is added and the fermentation takes place. The must ferments with the skins and seeds for ten to fourteen days at room temperature. The skins and seeds add tannin, color and complexity to the wine. After this, the red wine must is pressed and the pure wine is separated from the skin and seeds. We feed the processed skins, seeds, leaves and stems to our horses and they love it."

"During fermentation the wine is transferred from tank to tank several times, filtering and separating the sediment from the pure juice. The wine is stored for aging in cool tanks and oak may be introduced for flavor. The wines are bottled and often aged in the bottles as well."

Some of the wines have intriguing names, based on characters from the historic West, including **Outlaw Red**—a ruby red wine with the taste of black pepper, raspberries, spices and toasted oak. The name is explained on the label through this legend: "a descendant of the early Californian vaqueros, that Outlaw Red was formed and tested in the rugged red rock country near Moab. It's the world of Butch Cassidy and the Sundance Kid and life there forges individuals of steel and stone…where the old boys tell their exaggerated tales as they feel the presence of Outlaw Red."

The women of the Wild West are honored with a label named **Lily Rose White**—a wine that is golden straw in color with flavors hinting of apples, pears, cinnamon and honey. Based on another legend: "Lily Rose appeared like scented smoke in a red rock canyon. Her heritage was unknown, possibly even to her. Let it be said that she was always mysterious. While city boys admired her great legs, it was the country folk that could see the hybrid vigor that exploded from time to time, and gave special life to her calm demeanor."

Other popular wines include **Chenin Blanc**—a white wine that is fresh and light, with a fruity bouquet and flavors of apple, citrus and spice; **Pinot Noir**—a ruby red wine with a toasty berry bouquet and a fresh, spicy flavor; **Merlot**—a wine with a deep red color, smooth and mellow, with a hint of black currant bouquet; and **Cabernet Sauvignon**—a dark red wine with aromas of wood, sweet berries and pepper.

In addition to daily wine tasting, visitors are welcome to take part in many activities including mountain biking, whitewater rafting and kayaking, road biking, hiking and horseback riding. Overnight accommodations are offered in riverfront cabins and dining is available at the Cowboy Grill. Not to be missed is the Movie History Museum, open daily, containing hundreds of historical movie-making memorabilia items.

Castle Creek Winery at Red Cliffs Ranch is located at mile marker 14 on highway 128 northeast of Moab, Utah. A trip to Red Cliffs Ranch, a continuously operating cattle and horse ranch, provides an opportunity to be immersed in the culture of the Old West and learn about the New West. At Castle Creek Winery, where grapevines, cattle and horses share the red rock canyon, guests can share an appreciation for western tales and trails. ✾

COLORADO

CLOUDS BILLOW UP BEHIND THE CLIFFS OF THE COLORADO
NATIONAL MONUMENT, PROVIDING THE BACKGROUND FOR
THE PATIO, WHERE DOZENS OF WEDDINGS AND OTHER
EVENTS ARE HELD EVERY SUMMER AT TWO RIVERS WINERY.

THE TASTING ROOM AT TWO RIVERS WINERY.

Two Rivers Winery and Chateau
Grand Junction, Colorado

Two Rivers Winery and Chateau is set among rows of grapevines, flanked by the watercolored cliffs of the Colorado National Monument. Its seemingly perfect location is on the southwest side of Grand Junction, a city named for the confluence of two waterways, the Colorado and Gunnison Rivers. But, the stone buildings, reminiscent of a French Chateau, nor the vineyard, almost didn't rise there. Owners and founders, Bob and Billie Witham, originally planned to build a gated community of up-scale patio homes on the 15-acre site.

"It was never a life-long dream of ours to establish a vineyard and winery," Bob Witham said. "I had served for many years as the administrator of a company that operated 280 nursing home facilities throughout the United States. We were living in Texas and wanted to move back to Colorado where both sets of parents had retired. We thought the idea of building patio homes would be great for Grand Junction," he said.

However, the Withams were unable to obtain the proper demographic information to prove the area would be feasible for marketing luxury patio homes. Serendipity stepped in to move the Withams in an entirely different direction. "The day we decided not to embark on the patio home project was the day we tasted some Colorado wine that we didn't think was very good," Bob said. "I thought if this area could grow outstanding peaches, why couldn't it grow good wine grapes?" One of Bob's earlier jobs had been to guard the presidential and vice presidential airplanes. He said the food aboard the planes always included "absolutely delicious peaches from Palisade, Colorado."

After conducting some research, Bob found that there were several grape growers in the area, and the Colorado State University Extension Service was very cooperative in helping people to establish vineyards. Since both Bob and Billie had strong backgrounds in writing business plans, they set about developing a plan for a vineyard and winery.

ROBERT WITHAM, CO-OWNER OF TWO RIVERS WINERY, POURS A GLASS WINE FOR HIS DAUGHTER, BRITTANY WITHAM-CROWELL, TASTING ROOM MANAGER AT TWO RIVERS WINERY.

"We wanted to be hands on, so we rolled up our sleeves and got to work," Bob said. The first hurdle to clear was convincing the city council to approve a zoning change from residential to agricultural. They were successful in obtaining a Planned Unit Development license, a plan for a project that does not fit the pattern of the area. "The neighbors were very receptive to our idea, though, and it was fairly easy to get the change approved," Bob said.

The Withams worked with a college student to computer design the buildings, and they hired a homebuilder, rather than a commercial builder, to put the project together. Bob said a homebuilder is able to make on the spot changes more quickly than a commercial builder.

Following the design phase, it was time to plant grapes. They ordered 9,300 grapevines from the state of Washington. "They came on a UPS truck and we recruited family and friends to help plant the vines. We spent three days planting, with two of those days covering us with snow in a spring blizzard, so we wondered what the heck we were doing," Bob said.

After the grapevines were planted the Withams constructed the winery, their home and a tractor shed. "The winery was finished just in time for harvest, and we began making wine from grapes we purchased from other growers," Bob explained. They produced 1,200 cases of wine the first year, in 1999; then, by 2007, they increased production to 14,000 cases. The Two Rivers Winery currently makes about 15 percent of their wine from their estate grown grapes, and the rest from contract vineyards in western Colorado.

Once the winery was producing, the Withams turned their attention to marketing and brand recognition. They felt it was very important to have a tasting room where visitors could sample their wines. They had visualized from the beginning that they would have a conference center and country inn. "We wanted people to taste our product in a comfortable setting and in a celebratory fashion," Bob said. "We also felt it would be helpful to offer people a destination, and we've become very successful in presenting a total package to visitors. We were able to show a positive cash flow in three and a half years."

The Two Rivers Winery & Chateau brochure states—"Our wine country inn was created with the architecture and décor of a French Country Chateau. Our commitment to detail and the highest quality is evident throughout this beautiful and elegant facility, from the Australian brush boxwood-floored great room to the hand-painted murals on the surrounding walls and spacious sleeping rooms with elegant French furnishings and luxury bathrooms. Each of our ten large sleeping rooms has a distinct character, with names like Beaujolais, Burgundy and Champagne. And each room has wonderful views of our vineyards and the surrounding western Colorado scenery that can only be described as dramatic and inspiring."

The Chateau also serves as a conference center that can accommodate up to 150 people in the 5,000-square-foot great room. In addition, there are smaller conference rooms, an outdoor terrace and an outdoor pavilion available for groups. The facility has become a popular place for weddings, with 65 weddings taking place there in 2007. Other gatherings include concerts, picnics and reunions. The Withams often host non-profit groups at the Chateau and offer the use of the conference room on a complimentary basis. "We believe in giving back to the community," Robert said.

The success of the vineyard, winery and events are due to the efforts of the competent staff at Two Rivers Winery, according to the Withams. The staff includes Robert Witham, owner, a native of the western slope of Colorado, who is responsible for the day-to-day operations for Two Rivers Winery. Billie Witham, co-owner, is also a native of the western slope of Colorado. She is responsible for the financial aspects of the business and oversees the Chateau and tasting room operations.

Rob Hammelman serves as the winemaker. He grew up in St. Louis, Mo., graduated from Colorado State University, and earned a post-graduate diploma in enology (the science of winemaking) from the University of Adelaide in Australia. He returned to Colorado to become the winemaker at Two Rivers Winery, having learned the virtues of creating French-inspired wines, with complex earth and spice notes, and the technique of creating fruit-forward Australian style wines.

Rob Crowell is the special projects manager and manages the beverage activities at the Chateau. He is married to Brittany, the daughter of Bob and Billie. Brittany Witham-Crowell is the tasting room manager and weekend events coordinator for the Chateau, while Brandon Witham is the manager of sales and marketing, and responsible for the wholesale and retail outlet sales throughout Colorado.

Additional staff members have helped Two Rivers Winery and Chateau to become one of the premier destinations in western Colorado, offering wines of distinction. The varieties of wines produced at Two Rivers are few in number, but superb, according to its customers.

"Winemaker, Rob Hammelman, is very focused on producing only the best wines. By just producing five varieties, we are able to give more attention to the details, thus achieving consistency and predictability with each release. We use both traditional and modern technology to create a product that is a joy to drink. The wines at Two Rivers are fermented in stainless steel tanks and some are aged in three different types of barrels, American, French and Hungarian oak," Bob Witham said.

Two Rivers wines have garnered more than 95 medals in International Competitions, including the Pacific Rim International, the Grand Harvest Awards, the Southwest International, the Eastern International, Los Angeles County Fair, the San Francisco International and the Monterey Peninsula International. The wines include **Chardonnay**, a wine highlighted by the intense fruit of spiced apple and lemon custard, with subtle chocolate sweetness; **Merlot**, a wine with true finesse and elegant aromas of red berries, violets, and vanilla bean; **Syrah**, a wine with deep aromas of blueberry and blackberry with truffle, caramel, mocha and espresso flavors; **Cabernet Sauvignon**, a wine with complex aromas of mint, clove, nutmeg and cigar box that complement the blackberry and black currant fruit flavors; and **Riesling**, a wine that braids ripe fruit, blossoms and nectar with crisp verdant acid.

Guests are sure to experience a grand adventure while visiting Two Rivers Winery and Chateau. The estate is worthy of its location, standing proudly between the gateway to the Colorado National Monument and the Grand Valley of the Colorado River. ❦

THE BOOK CLIFF FORMATION FORMS A SOARING BACKGROUND FOR THE VINEYARDS AT GRAND RIVER VINEYARDS AND WINERY.

A SIGN WELCOMES VISITORS TO GRANDE RIVER WINERY.

GRANDE RIVER VINEYARDS
Palisade, Colorado

There is a symphony of sight and sound swelling to a grand finale beneath the soaring cliffs of the Bookcliff mesa, lending an aura to the name of one of Colorado's largest and grandest vineyards, Grande River Vineyards. Nestled beneath the 2,000-foot buttes and mesas that radiate warmth down to the vines, the grapes of this Palisade vineyard ripen to perfection under a harvest sky.

Perhaps this symphony was born from the blended family, dreams, and hard work of owners, Stephen and Naomi Smith. Stephen Smith worked in the oil and gas business for many years before following his dream of growing grapes and making wine. He and two friends made homemade wine in 1986, but found it was difficult to obtain Colorado-grown grapes. Stephen bought land in the Palisade area in 1987 and planted five acres of grapevines. He closed his Denver office, moved to Palisade in 1989, and made wine with one-third of his first crop. Smith loved working on the land and found the vineyard and winery business, along with promoting Colorado agriculture and tourism, to be very exciting.

"I feel it is so important for people to understand that we can't afford to let our food growing and agriculture enterprises in this country die," Stephen said. "People seem to be interested in getting back to the land and learning about agriculture. Hosting visitors in the winery is one way to educate them about food crops," he added.

Naomi Smith contributed to the symphony at Grande River Vineyards with a background steeped in the arts. She studied fine arts and spent several years creating pottery. Naomi worked with the Colorado and Grand Valley Children's choirs for many years, and served as the manager of the Grand Junction Symphony for ten years.

Stephen and Naomi blended their families together with four children, two boys and two girls. Naomi also blended into the winery business in 1994 by taking viticultural classes from the University of California, Davis; then managing the marketing end of the business. She's especially fond of hosting the many concerts held each summer

NAOMI AND STEPHEN SMITH, OWNERS, RELAX ON THE PATIO OF THE GRANDE RIVER WINERY NEAR PALISADE, COLORADO.

on the lawn at Grande River Vineyards. Naomi also serves on the board of Wine America, a national trade association.

"It's been so inspiring to work with winemakers at all levels of the business," Naomi said. "We need all levels of winemakers, from small vintners to large enterprises. So many more people are willing to try wine in the last few years, and we feel like we have made a real effort to bring wine to the people," she added.

Stephen explained the idea of growing grapes and making wine in western Colorado began with a clue from the past. "Around the turn of the century, nearly 50 farms produced nearly 1,800 gallons of wine, but Colorado went dry in 1916, four years before national prohibition. After that the vines were destroyed, but western Colorado's moderate winters and arid climate make for near-perfect grape growing conditions. A group of visionaries decided to return the vineyards to the area in the late 1960's," he said. With help from Colorado State University, several test vineyards were planted and some individuals began to grow grapes. The Colorado wine industry grew from only a few vineyards in 1970 to more than 60 by 2007.

COREY NORSWORTHY,
WINEMAKER AT GRANDE RIVER
VINEYARDS, PUNCHES DOWN THE
CAP ON A VAT OF FERMENTING
GRAPES AT THE WINERY.

Grande River Vineyards expanded into two farms, consisting of 80 acres of grapes, under the vineyard management of Jim Mayrose, producing from seven to eight thousand cases of wine a year. In 2007 the Smiths held an auction and sold some of the vineyard land to other farmers, then contracted to purchase the grapes from these farmers. They also sold a parcel of land next to the winery that became the home of the Wine Country Inn in 2008. The wine-themed inn is located near orchards, wineries, shops and galleries.

The only vineyard currently under the ownership of Grand River Vineyards is a demonstration vineyard located next to the winery. The grape varieties grown there include Merlot, Cabernet Sauvignon, Cabernet Franc, Syrah, Viognier, Chardonnay, Sauvignon Blanc, Semillon and Petit Verdot.

"For those visitors who enjoy noting the differences in leaves, cluster, habits and tastes of the classic European grape varieties, we have provided the demonstration plot so that people can see the many different varieties of grapes, be able to walk among the vines, and see and touch the plants," Naomi said. "We planned to just let the birds eat the fruit, but in November of 2003 it got very cold very quickly and the grapes froze. I said 'let's make ice wine.' Stephen didn't really want to make ice wine, but I thought it would be a real novelty. We ended up picking the grapes in the middle of the night in freezing temperatures. And, we made lovely wine that sold for $75 a bottle."

Stephen noted that from 1989 to 1991, the fruit industry in western Colorado suffered three years of hard freezes that destroyed a number of the grape and other fruit crops. "The fruit crops have recovered but are always subject to the whims of nature," he said.

In addition to its recent notice as a prime grape-growing region, Palisade is known at the peach capital of Colorado. Other fruits that are prominent include apples, apricots, cherries and plums. High desert and the towering backdrop of the Bookcliff and Grand Mesas encompass Palisade, situated at the east end of the Grand Valley. Warm winds, a temperate climate, and soils deposited by the Colorado River provide perfect growing conditions for many crops.

As James Mayrose, former vineyard manager, noted in a newsletter article, the vineyard management included irrigation and netting for birds. He said that in the late summer, as the grapes change color and the sugar levels start to climb, birds become interested in making a meal of the fruit. Under Mayrose's management all vine rows received a bird net cover to protect them from the hungry birds. A device attached to the front-end loader of a tractor allows the application of the netting, mounted on a long spool, by unrolling the spool onto the trellis, as the tractor drives the row. Before harvest, the same machine will retrace these steps and reverse the hydraulic motors, winding up the netting for storage until next year.

As harvest approached, it had been Mayrose's challenge to move the crews and machinery between the vineyards in order to pick each grape variety at just the right time. In a normal year harvest usually begins around the first of September and takes a month or more to complete.

When the harvest is complete, it is time for the winemaker and his assistants to take over. In 2004, Corey Norsworthy of Adelaide, Australia, joined the crew as an assistant winemaker at the Grande River Vineyards winery. Corey has experience working at wineries, retail shops and restaurants; and holds a degree in Wine Marketing from the University of Adelaide, Australia.

Corey works in the winery with state-of-the-art equipment including several large stainless steel tanks for fermenting, hundreds of oak barrels for aging, and an eight-spout bottling and corking machine. Corey loves working with grapes and says, "You have to be passionate to make wine."

Some of the passionate wines available at Grande River Vineyards include **Sauvignon Blanc,** a tart dry wine in New Zealand style, with flavors of green apples and citrus; **Meritage White,** a balanced blend of white Bordeaux varieties, Sauvignon Blanc and Semillon, fermented and aged in oak barrels; **Viognier,** made from a rare white grape originally from the Northern Rhone Valley of France, with the flora, spicy aromas and flavors of pineapple, lemon, kiwi, melon, honey and anise; **Syrah,** made from an ancient red variety of the Northern Rhone Valley of France, with black cherry, black pepper, chocolate, cinnamon and mint flavors. **Meritage Red is** the winery's flagship red wine, a blend of full-bodied Cabernet Franc, Cabernet Sauvignon and Merlot, the red varieties of the Bordeaux region of France. **Reserve Merlot** is a medal winner containing bouquets of cherries and plums with soft tannins followed by a smooth finish. **Reserve Cabernet Sauvignon** is a double gold winner, with notes of chocolate and blackberry and a lingering finish of raspberry. **Desert Blush** is a popular wine with a versatile, off dry flavor and is the color of a western Colorado sunset.

In addition to wine tasting at Grande River Vineyards, visitors are encouraged to learn about the process of growing grapes and making wine. "Even non wine drinkers are able to learn a great deal about agriculture in Colorado by visiting our facility," Naomi Smith said.

Grande River Vineyards is proud to participate in the Colorado Mountain Winefest each September. They are also excited to present many concerts throughout the summer season, where they often donate concert proceeds to charitable projects throughout the Grand River Valley, Colorado and the nation.

Visitors may walk among the vines and marvel at the towering cliffs guarding Grande River Vineyards. Listen, there's a symphony of amber leaves blowing in the breeze, melodies flowing from a crystal wine glass. ❧

WINE BARRELS FORM ATTRACTIVE
LANDSCAPING AT COLORADO CELLARS.

STARLEY TALBOTT

Colorado Cellars
Palisade, Colorado

Colorado's oldest contemporary winery is set in the Grand Valley of the Colorado River in western Colorado. The grapevines of Colorado Cellars thrive at a high altitude on the gentle slopes of East Orchard Mesa, overlooking the valley floor.

Colorado Cellars was first called Colorado Mountain Vineyards when the infant grape and wine business was born in Denver. Jim Sewell and Gerald Invancie founded the modern-day Colorado wine industry in 1978, as hobby winemakers, using grapes from California. Sewell and Invancie then moved the fledgling enterprise to Palisade, where they grew their own grapes for wine.

At the same time, Rick Turley traveled the highways of Colorado as a wine salesman. He also owned a vineyard near Palisade and sold his grapes to Colorado Mountain Vineyards. "Somehow, I convinced myself I wanted to own a winery," Rick said. "In 1989, when Colorado Mountain Vineyards refused to buy my grapes, I asked them if I could buy their winery, and they accepted my offer." Rick and his wife, Padte, set about expanding the vineyards to 450 acres and re-named the business Colorado Cellars.

"It took a few years for us to make a profit, but we do this for our living, and we've never regretted the decision to buy the winery," Rick admitted. Padte became the winemaker and Rick manages the vineyard, marketing, and deliveries.

The original winery building remains nestled in a hillside overlooking the Bookcliff Mountains, with the Grand Valley and the Colorado River stretching out below. The vineyards slope gently to the north and visitors can admire the view from a covered picnic area set amongst thousands of grapevines.

In 1988 the winery was completely renovated and expanded in order to accommodate the fermentation and storage of more than 10,000 cases of wine produced there annually. The fermenting tanks are all stainless steel and some of the wines are aged in oak barrels. The Turleys have retained some of the original equipment, such as an old basket press, which can be viewed on a winery tour.

RICK TURLEY DISPLAYS AN ANTIQUE WINE PRESS AT
COLORADO CELLARS NEAR PALISADE, COLORADO.

They replaced the old press with a six-ton bladder press they purchased from Fetzer Vineyards in California.

Turley said the vineyards are sheltered from the prevailing western winter winds and storms, due to an inversion effect created by the 10,000-foot high Grand Mesa dominating the eastern end of the Grand Valley. The Bookcliff and Umcompahgre mountain ranges on the north and south further protect the vines from harsh winter temperatures. With the valley open only to the west, the worst summer winds and storms are driven up and over the valley, leaving cool, dry nights and hot, dry days—just what grapevines need.

Grapes thrive in the valley due to the mostly deep clay-loam layers of soil, with underlying seams of sand that facilitate drainage. Virtually all Grand Valley vineyards are irrigated, thereby allowing the vintners control over vine vigor and fruit maturity, according to Rick Turley.

Rick and Padte believe in "hand made" wines and insist upon minimal handling and processing, thereby allowing the grapes distinctive qualities to emerge in the award winning wines of Colorado Cellars.

All grapes are hand picked at harvest time. "We've had some of the same crew for twenty years and some of them are more than 70 years old. They often pick fruit in the nearby orchards, too," Rick said. The Turleys also employ two additional full-time workers, including the tasting room manager, Cheri Smedly, who has been with them for 23 years.

Colorado Cellars currently produces 22 wine flavors including **Chardonnay**, fruit flavored with a toasty oak nose; **White Riesling**, complex peach and apricot flavors; **Orange Muscat**, lush, sweet, complex spicy orange flavors; Peach, tree ripened peach flavor and a crisp finish; **Roadkill Red**, unique, semi-sweet with raspberry overtones; and **Great Catherine's Spiced Mead**, honey wine reminiscent of apple pie or spiced cider.

Rick Turley says, "No we don't have a favorite wine, just as we don't have a favorite child. We don't have a signature wine, either. We believe all our wines are special, and it's up to the customer to determine their own favorites."

Wine is dispensed in the attractive tasting room, where a row of wine bottles contain specialized spouts for pouring. The area is chocked full of additional cooking products and wine foods including Zinfandel Garlic Salsa, Zinfandel Orange Mustard, Merlot Barbeque Sauce, Chardonnay Raspberry Fudge Topping, Pinot Noir Chocolate Cherries, and herbal cooking wines. There are also apparel and household items ranging from aprons to candles. Winery events include tours and wine tastings every day year round except Sunday, seasonal weddings, sunset dinners, concerts, and family events.

Rick Turley still travels thousands of miles each year promoting and selling the wines of Colorado Cellars. He's a sixth generation Coloradoan who reminisces about his great, great uncle, Simeon Turley, who was famous for making Taos White Lightning in the early 1800's.

More than a century after Simeon Turley made whiskey for Colorado's prospectors, trappers, traders and ranchers, his descendants are proud to be the owners of Colorado's original modern-day winery, Colorado Cellars. ✳

A SIGN GUIDES VISITORS TO CARLSON VINEYARDS ON
ORCHARD MESA NEAR PALISADE, COLORADO. THE
WINERY IS LOCATED IN AN OLD FRUIT PACKING SHED
AND THE VINEYARD WAS ONCE AN ORCHARD.

A VIEW OF CARLSON VINEYARDS.

CARLSON VINEYARDS
Palisade, Colorado

Laughter echoes from the walls of the old fruit packing shed, along a shaded lane on Orchard Mesa. Even the cats are chuckling at Carlson Vineyards, where the felines are made famous on several wine labels featuring a laughing cat. Then, there's the infectious smile and laughter of the owner and winemaker, Parker Carlson.

"We're not the swirl, sniff and spit crowd, when it comes to wine tasting," Parker said. "We're here to have fun and make wine tasting a fun experience for our customers."

Parker and his wife, Mary, moved to Palisade in the early 1980's and opened their winery in 1988, on an old historic farm that had once been an apricot orchard. For decades the Palisade area has been called the peach capital of Colorado, where hundreds of fruit orchards dot the landscape. Up on Orchard Mesa, overlooking the Colorado River, Parker Carlson was one of several new entrepreneurs who removed fruit trees and planted grapes.

Carlson began by planting Riesling grapes in his vineyard. A few years later he planted Lemberger, Zinfandel, Chardonelle and Orange Muscat grapes. He found the Zinfandel grapes didn't do well so he took them out. Eventually he decided to grow only three varieties—Riesling, Lemberger and Chardonelle. He also buys grapes and other fruits from local growers to be made into wine.

Carlson Vineyards are known for producing premium wines from the intensely flavored, sun-ripened fruits and grapes western Colorado is famous for growing. The best selling wine at Carlson Vineyards is not a grape wine at all, but a sweet and tart Cherry Wine that's touted as "cherry pie without the crust."

Cherry Wine also plays a part in one of the fun activities at Carlson Vineyards. Parker Carlson melts dark chocolate, dips a wine glass in the chocolate, allowing the chocolate to harden around the rim—then pours the glass full of cherry wine. "Guests just have a ball drinking the wine. They'll have chocolate dripping on their chins and they'll be laughing like crazy," Parker said.

VISITORS ARE OFTEN SURPRISED TO SEE NUDE PEOPLE WORKING IN THE CARLSON VINEYARDS, UNTIL THEY REALIZE THE FIGURES ARE MANNEQUINS.

Out in the vineyard the party continues. Several of the vineyard cats are roaming through the rows, occasionally stopping to stare at the nude figures standing discreetly among the grapevines. Visitors do a double take and figure they've stopped at the wrong place until they realize they're in on the joke. A mile north of the vineyard, one of Parker Carlson's humorous neighbors, Lyle Nichols, has placed a sign by the roadside reading, "Sunnydale Nudist Colony, one mile on the right." "People drive by very slowly, staring out the window, looking for the nudist colony. Most of them get a good laugh when they see that the nudists are really mannequins, and it's all in fun," Parker said.

Parker Carlson, however, takes the management of his vineyard and the wine making very seriously. He uses drip irrigation in the vineyard, very few chemicals and does not net for birds. "I let the birds have a few grapes, but we just don't have as many birds around as we used to," he says.

PARKER CARLSON DISPLAYS A FEW OF HIS AWARD WINNING WINES FROM CARLSON VINEYARDS.

Parker keeps his winery meticulously clean and says that is a big part of producing a good product. He uses polyvinyl tanks for fermenting and does not age any wines in oak. He took University of California, Davis, extension wine classes and did a "lot of reading and experimenting." He says he's made many mistakes and learned from them. "I've found you have to pay a lot of attention to detail when you're making wine."

Carlson also takes the marketing of wines and his association with other growers very seriously. He's a member of the Grand Valley Winery Association consisting of eight growers in the area known as the Grand Valley, which includes land in the valley traversed by the Colorado River in western Colorado. The Association consists of Carlson Vineyards, Canyon Wind Cellars, DeBeque Canyon Winery, Garfield Estates, Grande River Vineyards, Graystone Winery, Plum Creek Winery and Two Rivers Winery.

The Grand Valley Winery Association brochure explains that the area is renowned for its unique terrain, bright sunlight and excellent soils. The United States Government has named the Grand Valley an American Viticulture Area. This coveted honor is prized among wineries all across the country. The association member wineries are all located within a 12-mile area, offering a convenient tasting experience for visitors to western Colorado wineries.

The brochure also touts these facts—in 1974, the Colorado State University Research Center began a grape research project on Orchard Mesa; in 1977, the Colorado Legislature passed the limited winery act; in 1990 the Grand Valley AVA was approved; and from 1990 to the present time the wineries have continued to grow and produce fine wines.

Additional facts about Colorado vineyards and wineries are that it takes one ton of grapes to produce 150 gallons of wine, which equals 750 bottles of wine or 62.5 cases of wine. A typical Grand Valley vineyard produces three to five tons of grapes per acre. About 650 acres of grapes are grown in Colorado, and most vineyards are located in the Grand Valley.

Carlson Vineyards contains three acres of grapevines and bottles about 8,000 cases of wine each year. They employ four full-time workers and two part-time workers. Whoever is manning the tasting room, when visitors arrive, usually presents a short wine educational class along with the wine tasting. Carlson Vineyards have also been successful in winning many awards including a World Cup award from New York for the 2004 Riesling wine; and Best of the Fest, Colorado Mountain Wine Festival, for the 2006 and 2007 Gewurztraminer wines.

Some of the favorite wines at Carlson Vineyards include **Cougar Run Merlot**, a dry, medium bodied, full flavored red wine; **Tyrannosaurus Red Lemberger**, a dry, medium bodied wine with black pepper flavor; **Laughing Cat Riesling**—a semi-sweet wine with light fruity flavors; **Laughing Cat Gewurztraminer**, a semi-sweet wine with flavors of tropical fruit, honey and oriental spices; **Laughing Cat Sweet Baby Red**, a semi-sweet wine with fruity flavors, blended using Merlot, Cabernet and Muscat grapes; **Prairie Dog Blush**—a semi-sweet wine with big fruity flavors;

Plum Wine—a sweet-tart, spicy wine with flowery flavors and aromas; **Cherry Wine**—semi-sweet, like cherry pie without the crust; and **Fat Cat Muscat**—a sweet dessert wine made with Orange Muscat grapes.

Parker Carlson also likes to hand out recipes that include the use of Carlson Vineyard wines. Some favorites include Tyrannosaurus Red Spaghetti Sauce and Carlson Vineyards Sangria.

The crew at Carlson Vineyards invites visitors to stop by for a leisurely visit. It can be a bit tricky finding the winery because the numbered and lettered roads make several 90 degree turns every half-mile. Parker Carlson says, "If you think you've gone too far, keep going."

Parker is usually missing from the premises during the month of May when he goes fishing in Wisconsin. He takes along a few cases of wines that are then sold in five Wisconsin stores.

At Carlson Vineyards, perched high on Orchard Mesa, there are always a few cats performing their royal duties, while their human subjects go about completing the vineyard and winery chores. And, there's nearly always laughter permeating the clear air on a sunny Colorado day. 🐾

HIGH UP ON REEDER MESA, A SIGN
WELCOMES VISITORS TO THE WINERY.

KRIS VOGEL (RIGHT)
DISPLAYS BOTTLE OF
WINE WITH LABELS
SHE DESIGNED AT HER
REEDER MESA WINERY.

DOUG VOGEL
(LEFT) STIRS A VAT
OF FERMENTING
GRAPES AT REEDER
MESA WINERY.

STARLEY TALBOTT

REEDER MESA VINEYARDS
Whitewater, Colorado

A typical fall day at Reeder Mesa Vineyards might include punching down a vat of crushed grapes, feeding a herd of deer a few leftover grape skins, listening to elk bugle in a nearby Aspen grove, writing a newsletter or greeting guests. Doug and Kris Vogel, proprietors, enthusiastically welcome visitors to their cozy farm winery on the top of Reeder Mesa in western Colorado.

Doug, a former helicopter pilot, auto mechanic and cattle rancher, now devotes all his time to growing grapes and making wine. Even though he enjoyed raising Black Angus cattle he's somewhat fonder of raising grapes. "Grapes don't kick you and they don't get out of the pasture," he said.

Kris also enjoys her role in the vineyard and winery business as the tasting room manager, newsletter editor and graphic artist. Kris designs all the Reeder Mesa Vineyards wine labels, as well as designing projects for additional vineyards and other customers.

The Vogels planted 1500 Riesling grapes on Reeder Mesa in 1994 at an elevation of 5,600 feet. "We are 1,000 foot higher than most of the vineyards in the Grand River valley," Doug said. They found that the Riesling grapes do quite well at that altitude unless there is a late spring frost. "That frost happened in March of 2007, knocking down about half of our vines," Doug said. He added that most of the vines recovered but that production was cut in half for 2007.

The Vogels purchase grapes from other vineyards in Colorado and produce several wines from those grapes including Merlot, Cabernet Sauvignon, Chardonnay and Syrah. When Doug and Kris harvested the first crop of Riesling grapes in 1996, they sold most of the grapes. They also made a few gallons of wine for their own use and to give to friends and neighbors. "Most of the people we gave wine to really liked it and wanted to know where they could buy some," Kris said. That interest prompted the Vogels to open their own winery in the year 2000.

Doug took some University of California, Davis, wine making classes, read a good deal of information, and worked with some nationally-known wine consultants in preparation for becoming a winemaker. He's also very handy with tools, having been a mechanic. He set about building the winery and some of the machinery needed for processing wine. One of his unique inventions is a lift for hoisting wine barrels that he fashioned from an old wheelchair lift.

Doug ferments his white wines in stainless steel tanks and ages his red wines in oak barrels. He uses a mechanical crusher, a bladder press and a six-bottle mechanical bottling machine.

In the vineyard, Doug uses drip irrigation to water the vines that grow in the rocky, sandy and clay soil. His greatest problems in the vineyard are animals and birds. He has fenced the two-acre vineyard with an eight-foot-high fence to keep out the deer and elk. He uses noise, reflectors and cats to scare away the birds. He sometimes needs to spray sulfur to control powdery mildew but attempts to stay as natural as possible in his management practices.

Reeder Mesa wines have been the recipients of several awards including gold medals for the Land's End Red wine at the 2006 Colorado Mountain Winefest and silver medals at the 2007 Finger Lakes International Wine Competition and 2007 Southwest Wine Competition. The 2003 Merlot won a silver medal at the 2006 International Eastern Wine Competition and a silver medal at the 2007 Southwest Wine Competition.

The wines of Reeder Mesa have also been featured in several newspaper and magazine articles including: an article in the May 30, 2007, *Rocky Mountain News*, detailing the results of a Colorado versus California wine tasting, where many Colorado wines topped the California wines; the *Wall Street Journal*, in an article entitled "The United States of Wine;" and *Cowboys & Indians*, in July of 2007.

Some of the most popular Reeder Mesa Wines, residing in bottles labeled with picturesque scenes of the surrounding mesas, include **Vintner's Reserve Riesling**, refreshingly fruity and crisp, just off-dry in style; **Land's End Red**, a Bordeaux-style blend of three varietals, which were aged separately in oak barrels for periods of up to two years; **Blue Lake Blush**, made from the Shiraz grape. This blush wine is light, fruity and slightly sweet. The wine is named for the pristine lake nestled beneath the rim of the Grand Mesa and near a popular picnic area. **Land's End Wild Rose** is fruity, complex and bursting with cherry, strawberry and pepper taste. The wine is named for the picnic area/trailhead located on Land's End Road. It's a pristine area where wild roses and chokecherries abound. One can journey from the trailhead by foot or horseback into some of the most spectacular scenery in Colorado.

Doug and Kris Vogel often journey up Land's End Road and encourage others to do so, too. The road is located one mile from the edge of their property. "It's not for the faint of heart," says Kris, "But you'll never forget the fantastic scenery." The gravel road twists around 102 switchback turns to the top of Grand Mesa, the world's largest flat-top mountain at an elevation of 10,000 feet.

Travelers can also access the Grand Mesa on paved roads, where they will travel through four major ecological zones, to reach the mesa top that is covered with forest and more than 300 lakes. The Grand Mesa provides abundant hunting, fishing and other outdoor recreation. It also serves as a major watershed for western Colorado, sending its waters down into five drainage systems that support numerous orchards, vineyards, farms, and ranches. Recent archeological finds suggest that humans have traveled to the mesa top for more than 8,000 years to harvest the produce, game, and natural resources of the mesa.

Humans continue to enjoy the fruit of the harvests in the Grand Mesa area. Doug and Kris Vogel of Reeder Mesa Vineyards add to the joy of the harvest with their wines. The Vogels say, "since our tasting room opened in 2003, we have been so fortunate to meet and sip wine with so many wonderful folks from all over the country." 🎋

THE LEROUX CREEK VINEYARDS ARE BACKGROUNDED
BY THE PEAKS OF THE WEST ELK MOUNTAINS
NEAR HOTCHKISS, COLORADO.

YVON GROS AND JOANNA GILBERT, OWNERS OF LEROUX
CREEK VINEYARDS, POSE IN THE VINEYARDS.

LEROUX CREEK INN AND VINEYARDS
Hotchkiss, Colorado

A country boy from the French Alps and a city girl from New York City have found their heaven on earth—a vineyard in western Colorado. And, they are willing to share it with the rest of the world.

It seems that another Frenchman happened upon this same bit of paradise a century earlier, settled in the area, and named a stream Leroux Creek (*Leroux* in French translates to mean a light hue of red.) Years later, another man built some southwestern style adobe buildings on the land and opened the Leroux Creek Inn. Yet another man, Yvon Gros, purchased the property in May 2000.

Yvon Gros and his wife, Joanna Gilbert, hit the ground running, as they continued operating the Inn that May and began receiving guests immediately. They didn't slow down until October.

Since Yvon had been trained as a French chef and winemaker, he wanted to plant a vineyard and make his own wine. He and Joanna planted 4,000 grapevines in 2002 and proceeded to raise them using organic methods.

"Our secluded location on 47 acres reminds me of the Provence countryside of France," Yvon said. "It's definitely a place to renew your spirit. It's wonderful to work in the vineyard, and then to enjoy the fruits of your own labor with a glass of locally-grown and vinted wine," he added.

Joanna, raised in New York City, is equally enthralled with the Inn and Vineyard. She is a clothing designer and continued to fly back and forth to New York during the first years they operated the Inn and planted the vineyard. She is mostly retired from the clothing design business at present, but she's taken on a new venture—developing an all natural/organic skin care line using grape-seed oil, grape seeds, and wine from Leroux Creek Vineyards.

The vineyard is part of the West Elks American Viticultural Area, a nationally designated grape growing region. It is one of two regions in Colorado designated by the federal government as having unique geographic and climactic features that distinguish the qualities of a region's grape growing.

"This land definitely produces a high quality grape from which to make wine," Yvon said. "You can't make good wine unless you have good fruit to start out with. The grapes are my babies, and they are very happy here," he added.

"Our vineyard is in the high desert at 5,800 feet elevation," Yvon explained. "I irrigate the grapes by flood irrigation from a furrow. With the high, dry climate we don't have very many problems with pests or disease. I use a vinegar and water solution to control the weeds. Every little thing makes a big difference when producing wine. The process is very precise and intense," he said. Yvon keeps explicit written records for the vineyard that he says are very important.

"We also grow several different grape varieties in an experimental vineyard in cooperation with Cornell University in New York," Yvon said. His own favorite varieties are Chambourcin and Cayuga.

His son Dustin, who arrived in 2007, is very excited to be involved in the business, and is assisting Yvon in the winery. Dustin had been working as a sommelier (wine steward) at a restaurant in Philadelphia. The two men like "to keep the wine simple and make a product without using chemicals." They say the Chambourcin grapes are a challenge to work with but make a very good French-style wine. "It's especially delicious served with our local elk and bison meat," Dustin said.

Leroux Creek wines have an intriguing wine label featuring different drawings of frogs. Yvon said French people are often called "frogs" because they like eating frogs. "We don't mind them calling us frogs, and we thought we'd use frogs on our label for several different reasons," he added.

Joanna likes to tell the story of how the previous owner left a ceramic frog on the front step of the house, which she thought was very precious. She also told of visiting Yvon's Aunt Jane in France shortly after they had purchased the Inn. "Tante Jeanne was then 91 years old. She insisted on taking a whole bus load of people to eat at a restaurant in the Alps, where Yvon had grown up. We arrived at the restaurant and there was nothing but frogs on the menu. We ate frogs!!!" she exclaimed.

Joanna had Eileen Gallagher Jacobson, formerly of New York, and now a Colorado artist, design the frog labels for Leroux Creek Vineyards. "They're very whimsical and people get a good laugh when they see our labels," she said. "Now, people send us frogs from everywhere. We've got quite a collection," she added.

From frogs to vines, wines, lotions and French cuisine, visitors find a trip to Leroux Creek Vineyards a satisfying experience. Those who come to stay at the Inn are treated to a gourmet breakfast including fresh fruit or preserves from local farms and a special entree of Yvon's French creations. Dinner can also be arranged for parties of six or more and will include four to five courses of classic French Cuisine.

In addition to touring the vineyards and tasting wine, visitors are encouraged to participate in other activities in the area. Joanna says there is gold-medal fly-fishing in the nearby Gunnison River. Visitors may hike the West Elk Mountains or the Black Canyon of the Gunnison National Park. Biking is available along roads among orchards, mesas and ranches. Other activities include golfing, horseback riding, or floating and rafting nearby rivers. In addition to vineyards, the valley around Hotchkiss contains many ranches and fruit orchards of peaches, pears, cherries and apples. Fruit growers from the area have won numerous national awards for their luscious products. There are also several coal mines operating in the area.

It is said that the history of the North Fork of the Gunnison River valley was never really an Old West history of mountain gold rushes and gunfights in the streets. It's also said that history is only really just beginning in the North Fork Valley.

Part of that history is being made at Leroux Creek Vineyards. The country boy and the city girl have found their heaven on earth, where visitors are invited to share paradise with them. 🌸

THE WINERY AT STONE COTTAGE CELLARS WAS BUILT FROM STONES GATHERED FROM THE VINEYARD FIELDS.

THE WEST ELK MOUNTAINS FORM THE BACKGROUND TO THE FALL FOLIAGE OF THE VINEYARDS AT STONE COTTAGE CELLARS.

STARLEY TALBOTT

STONE COTTAGE CELLARS
Paonia, Colorado

Skiers often compete for awards on steep mountain slopes. In Colorado, not only skiers vie for medals by taking a snow-bound ride down a twisting pathway, but winemakers do it, too.

Twelve inches of snow, one November night a few years ago, made it impossible for a UPS driver to make it up the one-mile steep and winding gravel road to Stone Cottage Cellars Winery on Garvin Mesa. But winemaker Brent Helleckson was determined to get his wine to the UPS driver, so it could be entered in an international competition. Brent loaded the wine on a sled and skied down the road with his precious cargo.

"I tried to enter my wine in the 'Best Wine Delivered by Sleigh' category, but the judges didn't buy that," Brent related with a chuckle. Even so, one Stone Cottage wine won a silver medal and another won a bronze. No matter whether the wines garner medals or not, the Helleckson family works together in their five-acre vineyard near the top of Garvin Mesa at an elevation of 6,300 feet, a few miles outside of Paonia, Colorado. It's a labor of love for Brent and Karen Helleckson and their two children, Jacob and Stephanie.

The family spent 14 years removing and hauling stones from the vineyard site. The stones were used to build a cottage to live in, a winery, a tasting room, and an underground cellar. At the same time the buildings were being constructed, the family planted grapevines, nurtured the vines to maturation, and made wine.

Brent Helleckson was raised in Minnesota and became an aerospace engineer. Karen grew up in North Dakota and worked in marketing communications for a software company. The two met in college, married, and lived in Boulder, Colorado, for twelve years. "When the children were born, we decided we wanted to raise them in a more rural community, and we wanted them to appreciate the life that working on the land could provide," Karen said.

They bought property in the West Elks American Viticultural Area, a nationally designated grape growing area, near Paonia, Colorado, in 1994. Another Colorado grower had previously planted the land with Gewürztraminer and Riesling grapevines. The Hellecksons, however, re-planted most of the grapes—there had been seven acres of Riesling grapes that had never ripened. "The elevation is too high for Riesling grapes to grow well here," Brent said. They were able to keep the Gewürztraminer grapes and added Merlot, Chardonnay, and Pinot Noir vines, comprising the present vineyard of 6,000 vines.

"Our kids grew up in the vineyard—Stephanie learned to walk between the rows of vines," Karen said. Jacob loves to drive the tractor, mowing and tilling the land between the vine rows. The grape crop in 2007 yielded much less than usual, because of a late spring frost. There were only about 150 pounds of Merlot grapes, "too few to put them through the mechanical crusher and de-stemmer," Brent said. So the family processed the Merlot grapes by hand. The two teenage siblings hand de-stemmed Merlot grapes into a large metal vat, teasing each other, and singing songs with gusto.

The Merlot grapes would be blended with Gewürztraminer grapes to make an Alpine Dessert Wine. A previous batch of the dessert wine received many accolades at the 2005 Telluride Wine Festival. At the festival's winemakers' luncheon, hosted by wine experts, Doug Frost and Steve Olson, guests tasted several wines paired with each course of the meal. The Stone Cottage Alpine Dessert wine was chosen by nearly all of the 300 guests as their favorite wine served with dessert.

Other wines produced at Stone Cottage Cellars include Chardonnay, Syrah, Merlot and Gewürztraminer. These wines are fashioned using Old European methods and some are aged in fine French and American oak barrels. The aged wines are stored in oak barrels in the underground cellar, designed and built by Brent using innovative methods and re-cycled materials. The ceiling of the cellar was fashioned using an old metal grain bin from a North Dakota farm. The walls were constructed from rough-sawn aspen trees and the stone finish for the outside entrance came from the fieldstone found in the vineyard. Brent traded work with a man from a nearby coal mine to have a hole dug for the cellar.

"The temperature in the cellar stays very even, from 40 degrees to 68 degrees," Brent explained. "It can be 100 degrees outside and the cellar stays cool, or it might be ten degrees below zero outside and the cellar doesn't freeze."

Visitors might be surprised to find that grapes can be grown at such a high altitude in western Colorado. A mild climate in the area has allowed for dozens of fruit orchards to prosper. Some of the orchards were planted when the first settlers came to the area in the 1800's.

Fruits grown in the area are said to benefit from the rich soil, plentiful water and the "million dollar" pre-dawn breeze that keeps frost at bay. This breeze serves as a natural air conditioner—at night, warm air flows up from the lower valley and, by day, cool air flows down from the mountains. Peaches, apricots, prunes, sweet and sour cherries, pears and grapes grow on local farms.

Its founder, Samuel Wade, named Paonia for the peony roots that he brought with him by covered wagon in 1881. He submitted the Latin name for the flower, Paeonia, which was changed to Paonia by the post office. Paonia, where the original peony stock still grows in Town Park, is an active community abounding with music, art and theater. Celebrations include a spring Blossom Walk, July Cherry Days, an August Wine and Dine Weekend, a Harvest Festival, and a Wine Barrel Tasting on Thanksgiving weekend.

The Helleckson family is actively involved in promoting tourism and hosting visitors to their winery. Their goal is "to educate people about agriculture in general and remind them where their food is grown," Karen said. They usually host around three to four thousand visitors each summer, explaining how the vineyard is managed by using natural processes. They apply fertilizer to the vines from a nearby sheep farm; they flood irrigate using a ditch method; and they fence the vineyard to keep out elk and deer. The mature grapes are protected from birds by covering them with netting.

Years of hard work have brought satisfaction and joy to the Helleckson family, who invite others to join them in a quiet respite at the family vineyard and winery. Visitors may stroll in the vineyards, gaze at the mountains, smell the scent of wood and grapes in the cellar, touch the winery building's smooth stones, taste the wine, and savor the spirit of the moment. ❦

JOAN AND JOHN MATHEWSON STAND ON THE BALCONY OF THEIR HOME OVERLOOKING THEIR VINEYARDS AT TERROR CREEK WINERY NEAR THE WEST ELK MOUNTAINS.

WINE BARRELS ANNOUNCE THE ENTRANCE TO TERROR CREEK WINERY.

TERROR CREEK VINEYARD AND WINERY
Paonia, Colorado

The season's first snowfall in mid-October frosted the peaks of the West Elk Mountains and brought deer, elk, wild turkeys and bears to the lower meadows. The owners, John and Joan Mathewson, had completed the grape harvest at Terror Creek Vineyards. The grapes had been crushed and de-stemmed and were fermenting in large vats. The scent from the residue of leaves, stems and grape juice had brought the animals looking for a banquet. Joan had seen a bear peering in her kitchen window one day when she'd baked fresh brownies, and she'd found bear scat on the lawn the next morning.

The Mathewsons chose the Colorado mountain valley as a place to plant a vineyard, because it reminded them of the Swiss Alps, where they had once lived, and Joan had attended school to become an enologist. "Our steep southerly slopes, with their rocky, limestone soil, are ideal for growing grapes," John said. "We searched for a long time for the right place to plant a vineyard, and when we found this place, we knew it was the perfect spot," Joan added.

The couple had spent 26 years roaming the world while John worked in the global oil business. Their sons, John and Eric, grew up living in numerous countries and speaking several languages. "We developed a love for European wines," Joan said. "At the time, we didn't think there were any American wines that matched the European style. I'd worked in some of the vineyards in Switzerland, which deepened my interest in grapes and wine. When John had to go back to Saudi Arabia to work for a year, I decided I didn't want to accompany him, because I'd been there several times. It turned out to be the perfect time for me to attend school in Switzerland," Joan added.

She took a twelve-month course in enology (the science of wine making) in Changins, Switzerland, near Geneva. "We went to class from 8 a.m. to 5 p.m. every day of the week and worked really hard," she said. Joan graduated in 1986, and she and John bought the Colorado mountain property in 1987.

"I was used to working in the vineyards in Switzerland where the vine rows went nearly straight up and down steep slopes," Joan said.

"I get the feeling I'm back in Switzerland every time I drive up the steep road to Terror Creek Winery."

The winery's name comes from the snow-fed stream, Terror Creek, tumbling along the property's edge, where the vineyard is home to some of the world's highest-altitude grown grapes at 6,400 feet. "The earliest white settlers in the 1800's needed water for their crops and tried to tame the gushing creek coming down from the mesa-top behind our property. It's said that they called the creek a 'holy terror.' The name stuck, but was shortened to Terror Creek," John explained.

The Mathewsons planted 2,000 Gewurztraminer vines in 1989. They added a few more vines each year, reaching around 10,000 vines by 2007. They grow the varieties of Riesling, Chardonnay, Pinot Noir, and Gamay Noir, in addition to the Gewurztraminer. "Our hot sunny days, cool nights and low humidity create ideal growing conditions for producing premium-quality wine grapes," Joan said. "All of our wines are made exclusively from grapes grown in western Colorado," she added.

Even though Terror Creek has long since been tamed, and the Mathewsons irrigate their vineyard from its water with a sprinkler system, they are not without other challenges in the vineyard. They installed a 12-foot-high wire fence around the vineyard to keep out the deer, elk, and bear. They must install netting over the vines to keep the birds from eating the ripe grapes. They have very few problems with disease or insects. "We do have powdery mildew, as do most vineyards, and we spray a little for that," John said. "We try to keep to a minimum of using any chemicals in the vineyard," he added.

Their biggest challenge is the weather and every few years they get a late spring frost that damages the vines enough that they don't produce a good crop. "The vines are usually able to rebound and will grow again, but we don't have many grapes that year," John said. Such a frost happened, in the spring of 2007, leaving the Mathewsons with about half of their usual yield. The couple does most of the vineyard work by themselves, occasionally hiring part-time help, and recruiting family to help with the harvest.

After harvest, the grapes are de-stemmed and crushed. The red grapes are fermented with the skins on, but the white grape juice is pressed from the skins before fermentation. After fermenting in stainless steel tanks, depending on the style of wine to be made, the juices are snuggled in other tanks or barrels. "I age my white wines in stainless steel and never put any of my white wines in oak, though I do age my red wines in French oak barrels," Joan said.

"I make only dry wines in the Alsatian style," Joan explained. "The Alsatian style of wine making comes from the Alsace region of France, where mostly dry wines are made using a hands-off method. The wine is an expression of the grapes and the ground where the grapes are grown. Alsatian style wines are known for being bold and dramatic."

John has turned the early settler's underground food storage cellar into the wine barrel cellar. He constructed a convenient underground cement tunnel, leading from the fermenting room to the barrel room.

In a good year the Mathewsons produce around 1,000 cases of wine. Their wine is sold in a few stores in Denver and Boulder, but 80 to 90 percent is sold from the tasting room at the winery. "We get visitors from all over the United States and the world," Joan said. "We have some of the same people who come every year to purchase a few cases of wine. We are very proud of our Pinot Noir—a rich, fruity red wine—and believe it has a taste similar to that wine from the Burgundy area of France," she said. Other wines include a dry white Riesling that has a "smooth and supple taste;" a white Gewurztraminer that is "spicy and full-flavored;" and a unique white Chardonnay "vinted without oak and preserving all the delightfully fresh and fruity flavor of the grape."

From the nearby valley town of Paonia, it's a short drive to Terror Creek Winery. For flatlanders, the road to Terror Creek Winery can be a bit of a terror, but it's definitely worth the trip. Joan reminds drivers that "the vehicle going up has the right-of-way and those going down should pull over and stop to let another vehicle pass."

As the wines spend the winter aging, John and Joan Mathewson often take a little rest and relaxation by driving an hour and a half to go skiing. Living in Switzerland gave them a love for all aspects of mountain living. After a skiing break, they'll return to their mesa-top home, where they have one of the most picturesque views in the world. When spring arrives they'll be back in the vineyard and welcoming visitors to Terror Creek Winery. ❧

A COVERED BRIDGE OVER THE ST. VRAIN RIVER
WELCOMES VISITORS TO CIATANO WINERY IN
THE ROCKY MOUNTAINS OF COLORADO.

VISITORS MAY RELAX ON THE INVITING
GROUNDS OF CIATANO WINERY.

STARLEY TALBOTT

CIATANO WINERY
Lyons, Colorado

A tradition of Italian winemaking and family culture form the nucleus of Ciatano Winery, located in the foothills of the Rocky Mountains, near the little town of Lyons, Colorado.

When Mary Lou and Richard Gibson moved from Ohio to Texas, and then to Colorado, they never planned on opening a winery. They had traveled to Colorado on vacation and loved the "gorgeous scenery, especially the tranquil drive along the St. Vrain River, leading from Lyons to Estes Park and Rocky Mountain National Park," Mary Lou said. A few years later, when they had a chance to buy the Rock 'n River Bed and Breakfast on Highway 36, just over three miles west of Lyons, they decided it was a perfect opportunity.

Richard and Mary Lou, along with their four children, operated the Bed and Breakfast for ten years. "But several years ago, when gas prices started to go up, we realized we needed to add more incentives for people to travel to our area. We had a family meeting. Unfortunately, I left the room for several minutes, and when I returned my son, Guy, said, 'Mom's going to love this idea,' Mary Lou said."

The idea, it turned out, was to open a winery. Since Mary Lou's side of the family are Italians who had emigrated to the United States from Italy, the Gibson family thought it would be a unique way to honor their grandparents' heritage by starting a winery featuring Italian-style wines. "The kids said it would be easy, and all I'd have to do was serve wine to visitors and ask them if they were enjoying the wine," Mary Lou added.

Mary Lou soon found that operating a winery and tasting room was much more complicated than her children said it would be. At first they opened only as a tasting room, selling wines from other Colorado winemakers. But in 2002 they made some wine they thought was very tasty. Their customers liked it, too, and it was soon sold out.

They eventually hired Tim Merrick, of Trail Ridge Winery, just over the mountain on Highway 34, as their winemaker. Tim divides his time between making wine for his own winery and for the Gibsons. Tim has a small vineyard just west of Loveland, Colorado, but the majority of grapes for both Trail Ridge and Ciatano Wineries are purchased from growers on the western slope of Colorado.

By 2007, Ciatano Winery was exclusively selling their own wine. The Gibsons provided Tim Merrick with several of their old family Italian recipes for making wine. "There are times when we challenge Tim a great deal, but he always works with us and comes up with unique wines," Mary Lou said.

Mary Lou related the story of her Italian heritage and her grandparents—"Grandpa Donato arrived in America at age 12, from a small town in Italy's wine country, St. Bartolomeo in Galdo. He and Grandma Lucy settled in northeastern Ohio, in a small rural town they lovingly referred to as little Italy. The tradition of winemaking and family culture remained strong. Mother shared with us many wonderful stories of harvest and winemaking creating a legacy of handed-down, proud Italian traditions. We present our wines in their honor."

Mary Lou said that once Grandpa Donato had been arrested in Ohio for making illegal wine, but grandmother insisted the wine was only for the family, and Grandpa was released.

"I remember the wonderful family gatherings we had as a child. Every Sunday we'd have a huge family dinner with lots of wonderful Italian food, and, of course, lots of wine, too. Italian children are weaned from the milk bottle to the wine bottle. There was always lots of love and laughter in our family," Mary Lou said.

Even though Mary Lou's children are now scattered all over the country, she still honors the tradition of Italian cooking and Italian wines. "We have four children, Guy, Vernon, Nancy and James. We only gave Guy a name that could be translated into Italian, Ciatano, so the winery is named after him," she said. Guy lives nearby in Boulder and continues to assist in the winery. "And, I still cook food for Guy and take it to him. I tell him I'm his Meals on Wheels," Mary Lou chuckled.

Visitors to Ciatano Winery may participate in the Italian tradition of good food and good wine. The Gibsons sell picnic baskets loaded with gustatory delights, which can be enjoyed among the gardens and ponds that surround the winery or along the St. Vrain River that borders the property.

Ciatano Winery is located on the eastern edge of what was once the historic Hall Ranch. The property was the home of Arapaho and Cheyenne Indian tribes before the more than 20 different Anglo families lived and operated businesses at Hall Ranch. These families prospected, farmed and quarried sandstone. In the mid 1940's, Hallyn and June Hall bought the property and operated it as a working ranch for more than 50 years. Boulder County Parks and Open Space bought the bulk of the ranch in 1993, with the exception of the small acreage owned by the Gibsons. Those visitors that want to wander farther afield can hike over the hill at the back of the Ciatano Winery property, which leads to trails traversing the Hall Ranch open space.

The Hall Ranch is located at the interface between the mountains and the plains. The western portion of the ranch is made up of igneous rock formed eons ago. The eastern side is composed of red sandstone that has been extensively quarried. Many buildings in Lyons and Boulder were built using stone from these quarries. Hall Ranch consists of 3,206 acres of backcountry, providing wildlife habitat for many species, including raptors, birds, mountain lion, elk, bighorn sheep, deer, prairie dog, coyote, fox and rattlesnake.

On a tour of the winery, Mary Lou points out a cave cut into the hillside that serves as a wine cellar today. "It was once used to store apples. This whole area was known as Apple Valley and contained dozens of apple orchards," she said. Several apple trees still grow on the property, and Mary Lou said, "We often have a bear that comes to eat the apples, but he doesn't bother us and we don't bother him."

There are 18 acres for visitors to Ciatano Winery to roam—in addition to the winery there are picnic areas, trout ponds, a deli, gift shop and a spa. The deli features products from local vendors including smoked trout, cheese, buffalo and elk sausage and Italian gelato. Live music is featured each Saturday during the summer. In addition, there are four summer music festivals—a Jazz Fest in May, Grape Fest in June, Art Fest in July and a Car Fest in August.

MARY LOU GIBSON DISPLAYS WINE BARRELS IN THE WINE
CELLAR AT CIATANO WINERY NEAR LYONS, COLORADO.

All wines at Ciatano Winery are fermented in steel tanks and aged in oak barrels. The wines are bottled on a small machine, six bottles at a time, and are hand labeled. The wine labels include **Bianco**, a white Riesling; **Viognier**, a white blend; **Cabernet Franc**, a red varietal; **Syrah**, a red varietal; and **Vino Rosso Cambiani**, a red blend of three grape varieties.

Visitors will find much to admire at Ciatano Winery. The latest vintage of fine Italian style wines, the splendor of the Rocky Mountains, open space, wildlife, live music, and hospitality are a few of the amenities.

The motto at Ciatano Winery is *"Vi Buono Vino…Buono Vita!!!"* Translated to English it means *"Good Wine…Good Life."* That motto is lived in full at the winery on the banks of the St. Vrain River in central Colorado. ❧

AUGUSTINA'S WINERY
Boulder, Colorado

When life handed Marianne "Gussie" Walter a bunch of bitter grapes, she turned them into fine wine. Although it took a few years for Gussie to overcome the tragedy that took the life of her young, geologist husband, she eventually found solace among grapevines and in the solitude of her one-woman winery in Boulder, Colorado.

Gussie was also a geologist, with a chemistry background, and had made a few hobby wines that she liked. When her "life fell apart" following the death of her husband, all she wanted to do was "to get away for a while." She mailed some letters and knocked on a few doors, not really knowing what she wanted to do. But since she enjoyed the outdoors and wine, she left Boulder, Colorado, headed south, and was hired as an apprentice at Black Mesa Winery in Velarde, New Mexico.

"I did everything at Black Mesa, from picking grapes, to driving a tractor, crushing grapes, helping in the winery and bottling wine. I was hired because of my chemistry background so that I could assist in the laboratory. I did that, but I also gained valuable experience by helping out everywhere," Gussie said. Gary and Connie Anderson owned Black Mesa when Gussie worked there, but it has since been sold to Jerry and Lynda Burd.

Gussie stayed on at Black Mesa for a year-and-a-half. She then returned to Boulder, where she founded Augustina's Winery in 1997. Her business was the first licensed winery in Boulder. She operates the only one-woman winery in Colorado and says she is "probably one of the few in the entire world."

The winery is very low key and located in a small warehouse in north Boulder. It's known locally as the winery with the oddball art deco labels, fanciful wine names, and slightly different philosophy about wine. Augustina's is "dedicated to making wine that goes with backpacking adventures, raucous poker parties, family barbecues, good mystery novels, and gingersnaps," according to Gussie Walter.

In order to maintain her one-woman production facility, Gussie installed several small stainless steel fermenting tanks mounted on wheels, making them easy for her to move by herself. She also added a de-stemmer/crusher machine that can be rolled outside for crushing the grapes. The winery also contains a vertical style bladder press, a modest laboratory, and a one-bottle-at-a-time bottling machine. Gussie uses a pump and hose to move the grape juice from one tank to another. The pump is also used to move the juice into the American oak barrels that are used for aging and some fermenting of the red wines. Another piece of equipment is an old ice-making machine that was a gift. It is used to cool fermenting wines—one of the stainless steel tanks fits perfectly inside the icebox.

All of the wines at Augustina's are made from Colorado grown grapes, most coming from the western slope. "The day the grapes are harvested, I make the long, round trip to the vineyards with my old, ugly, but trustworthy 1979 U-Haul box van named Scud," Gussie said. "Once the grapes are back at the winery, I begin the process of turning them into wine—crushing and destemming the grapes, pressing the juice, preparing yeast cultures to start the fermentation, checking the chemistry, racking, fining and blending the wines. There is not a lot of romance in winemaking, no standing around in elegant costumes sipping wine from crystal goblets. Winemaking is mostly grunt work and then you clean the equipment, twice," she explained.

Gussie is most fond of making blended wines in a crisp, slightly acidic style with low residual sugar. She considers her wines to be table wines and makes no one-variety wines. She blends different grape varieties each season, depending on what grapes she is able to obtain.

"I make wine to go with activities, wine to drink at the table with dinner, but also wine to sip on the back porch or to savor by the campfire," she said. Gussie is known for her "WineChick" and "Backpacker" labels including **WineChick White**, an off-dry white wine with flavors of citrus fruits and spice—"best sipped while reading a trashy novel, or watching an old Cary Grant movie." **WineChick Blues** is a fruity red wine with flavors of blackberries that "goes well with chocolate desserts, most blues music, and all Chris Smithers tunes." **WineChick Red** is a dry, medium-bodied red wine that is "great for anything involving garlic, cheese, and friends making a mess in your kitchen." **Wine Chick Cherry** is a light, tart-sweet wine made from organically grown Colorado Montmorency cherries. **Boulder Backpacking Wine** is a dry, heavy-bodied red wine with dark berry flavors and a distinct smoky-herbal-earthy taste that is "best by the campfire after a day of backpacking." Another favorite and best-selling wine is **Harvest Gold**, a light semi-sweet white wine—"a wine for sitting on the porch with a friend, dissecting relationships, and listening to Jimmy Buffet tunes."

Her unique diamond-shaped labels, from her own idea, were developed by two Colorado artists—Brandy Lemae designed the WineChick labels featuring a stylized 1940's pin-up girl, and Byron Sina designed the Backpacker and Porch Wine labels.

Since the tasting room is tiny at Augustina's Winery, Gussie doesn't host many activities at the winery, but she takes her wine out to festivals and farmer's markets. A favorite is the Boulder County Farmer's Market, a large well-known market, held from April through October in downtown Boulder.

It is possible to visit the winery, by appointment, and sometimes individuals or groups "just show up," Gussie said. When her first batch of wine was ready for consumption, she'd been asked to host a group of nurses. "I was expecting three or four people, but they drove up in a van with 13 nurses, unloaded tables, mounds of food, and set up for a party. The party lasted several hours, while I mostly went about my work in the winery," she related. "Another time it was raining outside, so the visitors laid out a picnic lunch on the floor of the winery, amongst the tanks of wine, and had a grand time. That's what my wine is all about, having a good time," she chuckled.

Now re-married, Gussie and her husband, Dave Walker, are outdoors enthusiasts, who spend a month every winter backpacking and camping in countries throughout the world, while also enjoying the Colorado Rocky Mountains. With the exception of a month off in the winter, Gussie stays busy at the winery and taking her unique product to visitors at festivals and markets throughout Colorado.

Even though it's a great deal of work for one woman to juggle the tasks of winemaking, Gussie Walter has never looked back since she changed careers. She says "The pleasure comes from the creation of a product that is lovely to look at and drink. And if have a bad day, well, I can always have a glass of wine." ✤

JOHN DOMENICO BAKES PIZZA IN THE OUTDOOR OVEN AT
THE BALISTRERI VINEYARDS ANNUAL HARVEST FESTIVAL.

JOHN BALISTRERI, FOUNDER OF BALISTRERI
WINERY, POURS A TASTE OF WINE.

BALISTRERI VINEYARDS
Denver, Colorado

Untold numbers of feet have trod the soil on a small acreage in northeast Denver. Present day inhabitants know little of the people who once may have lived there thousands of years ago, but they know the feet that trod the land approximately one hundred years ago. The Balistreri family—Sicilian immigrants—came to Colorado in the early 1900's and established vegetable truck farms in a rural area near Denver. Some of their descendants planted flowers and opened greenhouses, making the acreage the largest producer of carnations in the United States by 1965.

John Balistreri, his wife Birdie, and their children, John, Ed and Julie added additional flower varieties. They worked seven days a week to supply fresh cut flowers to people all over the country, sometimes shipping as many as 10,000 flowers a day to their customers. However, the flower market in the United States dwindled after growers in South America entered the competition. By 1998 John Balistreri was forced to sell some of his land and enter into a new venture to make a living. He chose to plant grapevines to replace some of the flowers and to make wine. The greenhouse continued to operate along side the new winery but was finally closed in 2006.

"I'd learned to make wine from my uncle, and I made wine for years for the family to enjoy, so it seemed natural to start making wine to sell," John Balistreri said. John is the winemaker, Birdie helps in the tasting room, and daughter, Julie, is the all around person from helping in the winery and tasting room, to managing the business, to distributing the wine. Son John is a ceramic artist and professor at Bowling Green University in Ohio. Son Ed is a professor at the Colorado School of Mines in Golden.

"I'd always helped out in the greenhouse, so it was easy for me to transition to working in the winery," Julie said. "Though Dad told us running a winery would be less work than a greenhouse, it hasn't turned out that way. Now, we work seven days a week and nights, too," she said with a laugh.

Even though some of the Balistreri land has been sold, the vineyard and winery sit on a few acres in the heart of an industrial area of Denver. Warehouses and factories soon surrounded the farmlands that had once raised tons of vegetables, later flowers, and now a small vineyard. There are two acres of Cabernet Sauvignon and Merlot grapes, planted in 1996, four blocks west of the winery and tasting room. Some wine is made from the Denver vineyard, though most of the grapes used for Balistreri wines are produced in Palisade, Colorado.

Feet play a very important part in turning some of the Merlot grapes into wine. An annual harvest festival at Balistreri Vineyards each October brings hundreds of little feet to the winery grounds. The Merlot grapes are picked by hand from two different Palisade locations, Talbott Vineyards and Lovie Vineyards, put into square plastic field bins, trucked overnight to the winery, and then stomped by the feet of the many, many children who come to participate in the festival. The resulting juice is made into wine called "Little Feet Merlot," a favorite wine of many visitors. "When the children stomp the grapes, they really pulverize the grapes more than our electric crusher would grind them. The color extraction and big intense flavors are exceptional," John said.

An additional grape stomp at Belmar Festival Italiano in Lakewood also produces juice for the special wine. "Two different stompings with two grape sources are used to make two different Little Feet Merlots," Julie explained. "To help differentiate one from the other you have to look at the back label. It will tell you where the grapes were stomped and also the vineyard where they were grown. Though different from each other, both of the Little Feet Merlots have rich lush fruit flavors up front, with great tannin structure for balance," she added. When parents or grandparents pre-purchase bottles of the Little Feet Merlot, a portion of the sales is donated to The Children's Hospital Foundation of Denver.

All of the wines at Balistreri Vineyards are crafted in a unique style. "The grapes are fermented in the field bins they were picked into, everything goes into the bins, stems and all. We ferment the whole fruit," John said. "Fermentation begins using the natural, wild yeasts that are present in the air. We don't use any fining, filtering or sulfites in making our wines. After the initial fermentation is completed in the bins, we siphon off the free-run juice directly into American oak barrels.

The remaining must is placed in a bladder press to extract the rest of juice that is also placed in oak barrels. The wines are then aged in the barrels for one year. We then bottle the wine, directly from the barrel, using a small four-spigot bottling machine. We hand cork and hand seal with wax all 50,000 bottles that we now produce each year."

The wines of Balistreri Vineyards are big, full, and heavy-bodied with a fruit forward style. John likes the grapes to be very mature when they are picked and to test at a range from 26 to 29 brix (a measure of the percentage of sugar in grapes). Most of the wines have from 14.5 percent to 17 percent alcohol content. "Most tasters won't notice the high alcohol content, though, because the wine is smooth and complex," John said.

Most of the wines are sold directly from the tasting room, while some are featured in various retail outlets in Colorado. Wine is shipped to Wisconsin and sold in a few outlets there, because the Balistreri family has numerous relatives in the Milwaukee area.

Some of the wines include **Chardonnay**, referred to as "UnChardonnay" by the Balistreris because it is barrel fermented and is full of body and complex fruit flavors; **Dry Muscat**, the Balistreri traditional family wine, floral with clove and allspice overtones; and **Colorado Little Feet Merlot**, with juicy berry flavors and a hint of sweetness. **Syrah** wine is made from grapes grown at Horse Mountain Vineyards. It is intense with cream and berries up front, finishing with spicy black pepper. It won a gold medal at the Colorado Mountain Wine Fest, and silver medals at the Colorado Mountain Wine Fest, Tasters Guild International, and Finger Lakes International. **Colorado Cabernet Sauvignon** is made from Lovies Vineyard's grapes and has blackberry flavors, with spicy oak and vanilla overtones. **Colorado Cabernet Franc** is made from Whitewater Hill Vineyard grapes and has a ripe plum flavor, with hints of lavender and tobacco. **Colorado Cherry** wine is aged for 24 months in oak barrels. It has an almond, spice and strawberry aroma, with sweet cinnamon cherry flavor. It won a gold medal at the Colorado Mountain Wine Fest, silver at Tasters Guild International, and bronze at Finger Lakes International. John Balistreri imports a few grapes from Lodi, California, where his cousin owns a vineyard. These are used to make the Brothers Cabernet Sauvignon and Port wines.

A number of events are hosted each year at the Balistreri Vineyards including a spring barrel tasting and dinner, concerts,

A YOUNG GIRL PREPARES TO PARTICIPATE IN THE ANNUAL LITTLE FEET GRAPE STOMP AT BALISTRERI VINEYARDS HARVEST FESTIVAL.

A T-SHIRT AND SHOES ARE LEFT ON THE LAWN AT BALISTRERI VINEYARDS AS CHILDREN PARTICIPATE IN THE GRAPE CRUSH TO PRODUCE JUICE FOR THE LITTLE FEET MERLOT WINE.

patio bistros, a Labor Day customer appreciation celebration, and the October Harvest Festival. A highlight of some of the events includes pizza baked in the outdoor adobe and ceramic oven located on the winery grounds. John Balistreri, junior, designed the oven and constructed it with the help of his brother Ed and an uncle.

Visitors are often amazed to find the winery and vineyard just 10 minutes from downtown Denver, tucked between giant warehouses and factories, on East 66th Avenue. From big and bold wines, to home-baked pizza, to music, and hundreds of little feet stomping grapes, the trail to Balistreri Vineyards is worth finding. ✳

Spruce Mountain Meadery
Larkspur, Colorado

Nestled in pine-forested hills, on a quiet country lane, is the micro-winery of Spruce Mountain Meadery. Gretchen and Harrison Bliss are the proprietors of this unusual winery that specializes in the crafting of wine made from honey and called mead.

"We got our taste for mead-making while traveling and working in Europe," Harrison said. "We were fascinated by the many family wineries creating unique wines, and we loved the taste of the local mead. When we returned to the United States we had a difficult time finding mead in the stores, so we decided to make our own. It turned out well and when we shared it with friends, they always wanted to buy some. So we became licensed and Spruce Mountain Meadery was born," he explained.

HARRISON BLISS EXPLAINS THE METHOD OF MAKING MEAD, OR HONEY WINE, AT HIS SPRUCE MOUNTAIN MEADERY IN COLORADO.

The modest winery at Spruce Mountain contains four 1,0000 liter stainless steel tanks for fermenting the wine, a vessel for heating the basic mixture, a small bottling machine, various testing devices, stacks of boxes, and unique cobalt blue bottles containing the three types of mead produced there. Four more stainless steel tanks have been ordered from Italy and will add to the production line.

"Each of our meads is made from the finest ingredients available," Harrison said. "Mead is historically referred to as the 'nectar of the gods' or 'ambrosia,' and the essence of this nectar comes from the honey, water, fruits and spices that go into the mead. We pasteurize our meads to retain the essence of our ingredients, and we don't add sulfites to our product," he added.

The basic recipe for making mead, according to Harrison Bliss, is by adding three pounds of honey to one gallon of water, heating the mixture to 160 degrees for ten minutes, chilling the mixture, adding yeast, then fermenting the mixture for several weeks or months. The mead is then bottled and usually bottle aged for a few more months before selling. The meads crafted at Spruce Mountain Meadery are crafted to be "more on the dry side," Harrison said. "They are not a dessert wine and pair well with food," he added.

There are many kinds of honey, based on the flowers the bees collected nectar from. All of Spruce Mountain meads are made from clover honey obtained from an apiary at Lyons, Colorado. Harrison Bliss said one of the advantages to making wine from honey is that it can be made year round and is not dependent on the harvesting of grapes.

There is no formal tasting room at Spruce Mountain Meadery at the present time though tours are conducted by appointment, and the couple attends several festivals throughout Colorado. They competed in the 2008 International Mead Competition in Boulder, Colorado, with 130 entries from the United States, Canada, Poland and Slovakia. Spruce Mountain Meadery won a silver medal for their traditional honey wine and a bronze medal for the spiced wine. Future plans include the establishment of a larger winery and tasting room at a different location. Spruce Mountain currently produces 600 cases each year, and the wine is available at several local retail establishments.

The label on a bottle of honey wine from Spruce Mountain Meadery evokes the legends and lore surrounding the ancient and mysterious drink—"the stories of ancient mead come from the legends of Beowulf and Odysseus, Viking and Celtic lore, Shakespeare's sonnets, and Chaucer's tales. From ancient times, mead was shrouded in mystery and renowned for its gratifying pleasures. Reclaimed anew from the treasures of the ancients, mead is the stuff of legend."

Three types of mead are available at Spruce Mountain Meadery, including **Traditional Honey Wine**, a celebration of the delicate flavors and aromas of pure honey, crafted in the western European style of a dry wine; **Blackberry Honey Wine**, the subtle taste and aroma of honey combines with the intensity of blackberries to create a succulent wine to enjoy by itself or serve with a favorite food; and **Honey Wine with Cinnamon & Nutmeg**, this special festive mead combines the aromas and flavors of honey with the added richness of cinnamon and nutmeg to provide the perfect compliment to a cozy winters eve by the fire.

"The smell of pines, the rustle of aspens, the serenity of deep snow, and visits from the local wildlife create the perfect atmosphere for developing our exceptional meads," the Blisses say. Visitors to Spruce Mountain Meadery can live the legend and taste the "nectar of the gods." ❀

WINE BOTTLES AT THE WINERY AT HOLY CROSS ABBEY HAVE DISTINCTIVE CROSSES ON THE LABEL. SHOWN HERE, THE SIGN ANNOUNCES THE WINERY WITH THE ABBEY IN THE BACKGROUND.

MATT AND SALLY COOKSON, CO-OWNERS, STAND IN FRONT OF THE WALL OF WINES AT THE WINERY AT HOLY CROSS ABBEY IN CAÑON CITY, COLORADO.

STARLEY TALBOTT

THE WINERY AT HOLY CROSS ABBEY

Cañon City, Colorado

The spirit of Benedictine monks continues to reside at Holy Cross Abbey even though the monks no longer live there. That spirit proved to be a guiding light for Matt and Sally Cookson, who arrived in Cañon City, Colorado, in 2002, "on a wing and a prayer," Sally said. The Cooksons came to oversee the operation of The Winery at Holy Cross Abbey, and a few years later, along with partner, Larry Oddo, they became the owners and operators of the winery.

Holy Cross Abbey was established as a Benedictine monastery in 1886 and became an abbey in 1925. The monks served the people of Colorado by providing retreats and operating a high school until 1985. Reviving an earlier history of winemaking at the abbey, the monks planted grapevines in 2000 and soon began making wine. Their dream of operating a fine winery was realized for a few years, until the abbey was closed in 2004, though others carry their dream forward. The impressive Gothic-style abbey now serves as a community events center and is available for weddings, reunions, retreats and other events. The historic building is located close to the winery. Guests can visit the nearby tasting room or enjoy the spacious outdoor gardens, vineyard and picnic area.

A smaller building that serves as the tasting room was constructed in 1911, in the traditional arts and crafts style, according to Sally Cookson who serves as marketing and sales manager. Various owners used it for a home and a place to entertain guests, until it was acquired by the state of Colorado in the 1950's. It eventually was purchased by the abbey and in recent years had served as a rental house. "It was a mess when we came to Cañon City and the grounds between the winery and the abbey were filled with trash, and there was no grass there anymore," Sally said. "I was disheartened, to say the least, but we got to work cleaning the place up, and it was a joyous day when the sod was rolled out to make a park there. The first time I saw kids playing on the grass, I thought I'd died and gone to heaven," she admitted.

Matt Cookson is the winemaker and general manager and guided the formation of the winery and the development of fine wines "that everyone can enjoy," he said. Matt received his degree in enology (the science of making wine) from Fresno State University in 1984; then worked in New York and California, learning advanced winemaking skills. He perfected the art of creating some of the world's outstanding Merlot wines at St. Francis Winery in California; then worked at Robert Keenan and Rombauer wineries in Napa Valley before relocating to Colorado.

"We produce our wines using state of the art crushing, fermenting, and bottling equipment," Matt said. "We use ozone sterilization for sanitizing our equipment and oak barrels for aging most of the wines."

Approximately 750 vines grow in the vineyard next to the winery but are mainly used as experimental vines and to show visitors how grapes are grown. Most of the grapes made into wine at Holy Cross Abbey are transported in refrigerated trucks from the western slope of Colorado to the winery in Cañon City. Grapes produced by more than 30 local growers, however, are used to make an exciting community wine named Wild Cañon Harvest. This blush wine— a light, fruity wine—was developed when several local growers approached Matt Cookson with grapes to sell.

"They all had small amounts of grapes, so I thought it would be interesting to crush the many varietals together and see what happened," Matt said. What happened was a wine that won a gold medal and Best of Class at the prestigious Jerry D. Mead International Wine Competition in 2008. "This award really honors the people in the community who grew and cared for these grapes," Cookson said. The back label lists the people who delivered 19 tons of grapes in 2007. Because these growers help with the harvest they are called "The Wild Bunch." The label also mentions local 4-H and Girl Scout groups, who help pick grapes to raise money for their clubs.

The Winery at Holy Cross Abbey currently produces 12,000 cases of wine each year that consistently win awards in major competitions. **Colorado Merlot** is the signature wine made from grapes grown at Talbott Farms in Palisade. **Colorado Cabernet Franc** is a full-bodied wine made from grapes produced at Avalanche

Vineyards in Palisade. **Colorado Cabernet Sauvignon** is a wine with black fruit aromas, made from Talbott Farms and Whitewater Hill Vineyards. **Colorado Cabernet Sauvignon Reserve** is a finely crafted blend of Cabernet Sauvignon, Merlot and Cabernet Franc grapes, aged in oak barrels. **Wild Cañon Harvest** is a light, fruity wine, made from 21 different grape varieties grown by local growers. **Colorado Merlot Divinity** is a smooth and velvety after-dinner wine, made from grapes grown by Grande River Vineyards in Palisade. It was a gold medal winner at the Colorado State Fair.

Special events at the winery include the Spring Fling in March, Art on the Arkansas in June, and the annual Harvest Fest the last weekend of September. Visitors are also encouraged to visit many of the local historical sites in and around Cañon City.

Cañon City was founded in 1899 by gold and silver barons, who infused the city with their new-found wealth from the nearby mining camps of Leadville and Cripple Creek. Located along the Arkansas River, with three railroads, the city served as a transportation center and provided a pleasant place to live. Cañon City also became the home of the Colorado State Penitentiary in 1871. The only railroad remaining is the historic Royal Gorge Route, which carried passengers through the Royal Gorge along the Arkansas River beginning in 1879. This was one of the most complex railroads built in North America, with raging, class four and five rapids on one side and solid granite cliffs, towering more than 1,000 feet above, on the other side. The train now operates as a tourist train. Passengers stop below the famous hanging bridge, built at a point where the Gorge narrows to just thirty feet. The two-hour journey, covering twelve miles, can be taken aboard open-air cars. Some guests may wish to make the journey in the luxury of a dining car, where they can enjoy a meal and Colorado wine.

In addition to the Royal Gorge journey, visitors have other options for exploring in Cañon City. Several area museums include the Dinosaur Depot Museum, the Museum of Colorado Prisons, and the Royal Grand Railroad Museum. Outdoor activities range from rafting, to fishing, to hiking. A visit to the historic Holy Cross Abbey might include a stop at The Winery at Holy Cross Abbey for a taste of "divine wine." ❧

A SIGN GUIDING VISITORS TO GUY DREW VINEYARDS IS
A TRIBUTE TO THE MANY NATIVE AMERICAN ARTIFACTS
FOUND THERE, NEAR THE FOUR CORNERS AREA,
WHERE THE STATES OF COLORADO, UTAH, ARIZONA
AND NEW MEXICO FORM A COMMON BORDER.

AN AUTUMN VIEW OF GUY DREW VINEYARDS.

STARLEY TALBOTT

GUY DREW VINEYARDS
Cortez, Colorado

Following in the footsteps of Ancestral Puebloans, who farmed the Four Corners area of southwestern Colorado for more than 700 years, present-day farmers continue to work the land that provided sustenance to those ancient cultures. The landscape of rolling sage plains, rimmed by towering mountains and mesas, has drawn native peoples, explorers, and modern day settlers to the region for thousands of years.

Guy and Ruth Drew were drawn to the spectacular vistas and mild climate of the area when they moved to McElmo Canyon, southwest of the town of Cortez, in 1998.

They had searched for several years for property where Guy could fulfill his dream of "playing in the dirt." The land they found was located at 5,800-foot elevation, contained no buildings or other improvements, and had formerly been used to grow hay and apples.

As they began clearing and leveling the land, they found evidence of old ruins and artifacts. One major artifact they found was an arrowhead that eventually served as the pattern for the Guy Drew Vineyard's signs and labels. They also gained valuable information about farming the area from the clues left behind by former agriculturists.

"I learned two things early on in our project," Guy said. "The first is that the Anasazi (a Navajo word meaning ancient foreigners) knew the best places to grow food; and the second is that later farmers had found the best places to grow apple orchards. I learned to follow their discoveries to aid me in finding the best places to plant grapes," Guy said.

"One important facet for the vineyard was to learn how cold air works. We tried to plant our grapes in areas that have the minimum frost liability," Guy said. He planted six acres of grapes in 1999 to Cabernet Sauvignon, Cabernet Franc, Syrah, Merlot, Chardonnay, Sauvignon Blanc, Riesling, and Petit Verdot varieties. Guy usually places the vines in 500-vine blocks, on a half-acre for each block. By 2007 he had planted nearly 20 acres of vines at various locations.

GUY AND RUTH DREW WELCOME VISITORS TO THEIR
SPANISH STYLE HOME AND WINE-TASTING ROOM MADE
FROM STRAW BALES COVERED WITH ADOBE.

The vines are watered with a drip irrigation system and supported by a vertical shoot position trellis. At harvest time Guy has found the help of local Navajo women to be invaluable. "They are the best pickers around; they treat the grapes with tenderness, and yet they quickly complete the task," he said.

After the land was cleared and the vineyards planted, Guy built the winery, a home, and other buildings using straw bales covered with stucco. The buildings are finished in a southwestern pueblo style, complementing the history of the area. The Guy Drew Vineyard's brochure invites visitors to "capture the allure of our vineyards and straw bale winery, carefully situated among ancient dwellings, scattered along the historic trade route and fields of picturesque McElmo Canyon."

The ultra-modern winery contains state-of-the-art equipment including stainless steel tanks and an automated bottling machine. A separate barrel room (the only building that is not built of straw bales) holds hundreds of American and French oak barrels. The white wines are fermented in stainless steel and not usually aged in oak. Depending on the style, most red wines are aged in oak barrels from eight months to two years.

The barrel room is equipped with a misting system to keep the barrels at the correct temperature and humidity. The winery also has an extensive laboratory for testing the wine, which Guy says is "crucial to making good wine." From 2,000 to 5,000 cases of wine are currently produced, and plans include production of 10 to 15,000 cases a year in the future.

The Four Corners area is a new grape-growing region, having only one other vintner in the area before Guy Drew arrived. He says there are now more than ten other growers. "However, being a new wine area, it will take time to see how the grapes do and what works the best," Guy said. He believes it is a prime grape-growing area and could become Colorado's best wine region. "My goal is to help grow the industry here. We still have lots of suitable land that is still relatively inexpensive and we have plenty of water," Guy said.

Guy and Ruth host wine tastings in the cozy kitchen of their adobe home, where Navajo rugs adorn the walls and the couch of a corner breakfast nook. Ruth's artwork is displayed throughout the house, including rows of brightly painted gourds, visible through the open arch to the living room. The Drews often host tourism events and serve on boards aimed at bringing visitors to the Cortez area.

The southwest corner of Colorado is world-famous for the canyons and cliff dwellings of ancient peoples. Mesa Verde National Park, ten miles east of Cortez, is one of America's premier archaeological wonders. Hundreds of historic homes and villages have existed there for more than eight centuries, preserved and protected by overhanging cliffs. Sometime in the late 1200's, the Ancestral Puebloans left their homes and moved away. Local cowboys first reported the cliff dwellings in the 1880's, and since that time people have sought to understand these people's lives. They left no written records, but the structures they left behind give clues as to how they lived and farmed the area. They grew crops consisting of beans, corn and squash; gathered wild plants; and hunted deer, rabbits, and other game.

There are also several other notable historic sites in the area including Ute Mountain Tribal Park, Canyons of the Ancients National Monument, the Anasazi Heritage Center, Crow Canyon Archaeological Center, and Hovenweep National Monument. Visitors heading to Hovenweep National Monument from Cortez will drive right by Guy Drew Vineyards. They are invited to stop by for a tour and wine tasting.

The wines of Guy Drew Vineyards include **Cabernet Sauvignon,** a wine made entirely of fruit from McElmo Canyon, with aromas of dark fruits with nuances of oak, vanilla and light smoke. **Syrah** is a wine aged in French oak barrels for 15 months. It is medium-bodied with flavors of cherry, prune and raspberry. **Meritage** is a blend of Cabernet Sauvignon, Cabernet Franc, Merlot and Petit Verdot, barrel aged for 15 months. It combines dark fruit flavors, chocolate and leather notes with a hint of vanilla. **Gewurztraminer** is an off-dry wine with grapefruit, rose and citrus aromas and flavors of honey, fruit and spicy nutmeg. The grapes for this wine came from vineyards within 100 miles. **Cabernet Franc** is a wine with classic cherry aromas, aged two years in a combination of new and two-year-old French oak barrels. **Riesling** is the Guy Drew signature wine, with apricot, citrus, tangerine and green apple flavors.

At Guy Drew Vineyards, visitors can experience the ritual of historic agricultural traditions combined with modern methods. By traveling the trail of the Ancients, one might imagine how those venerable peoples lived under the same wide skies. ✻

Appendix

Vineyards and Wineries in New Mexico, Arizona, Utah and Colorado

This list is complete according to available information as of January 2009.

Please contact the vineyards and wineries ahead of your visit to schedule an appointment or inquire about hours of operation and obtain directions.

New Mexico

Anasazi Fields Winery: 26 Camino de los Pueblitos, Placitas, NM 87043; telephone (505) 867-3062; web site: www.anasazifieldswinery.com; e-mail: anasazifieldswinery@att.net. Contact: Jim Fish.

Anderson Valley Vineyards: 4920 Rio Grande Blvd., NW, Albuquerque, NM 87107; telephone (505) 344-7266; contact: Patty Anderson

Arena Blanca Winery: 7320 U.S. Highway 54/70, Alamogordo, NM 88310; telephone (800) 368-3081; web site: www.PistachioTreeRanch.com; e-mail: info@pistachiotreeranch.com. Contact: Tim McGinn.

Balagna Winery: 223 Rio Bravo Drive, Los Alamos, NM 88301; telephone (505) 672-3678; web site: www.balagnawinery.com. Contact: John Balagna.

Black Mesa Winery: 1502 Highway 68, Velarde, NM 87582; telephone (800) 852-6372; web site: www.blackmesawinery.com; e-mail: jer@blackmesawinery.com. Contact: Lynda or Jerry Burd.

Casa Rondeña Winery: 733 Chavez Road NW, Los Ranchos de Albuquerque, NM 87107; telephone (800) 706-1699; web site: www.casarondena.com; e-mail: info@casarondena.com. Contact: John Calvin.

Cottonwood Winery: 1 E. Cottonwood Road, Artesia, NM 88210; telephone (505) 365-3141; web site: www.cottonwoodwineryllc.com; e-mail: cottonwoodwino@pvtn.net. Contact: Dale or Penny Taylor.

Corrales Winery: 6275 Corrales Road, Corrales, NM 87048; telephone (505) 898-5165; web site: www.corraleswinery.com; e-mail: gr8wine@swcp.com. Contact: Keith Johnstone.

Falcon Meadery and Winery: 1572 Center Drive, Unit E, Santa Fe, NM 87501; telephone (505) 471-3432; web site: www.falconmead.com; e-mail: info-2008@falconmead.com. Contact: Darragh Nagle.

Gruet Winery: 8400-A Pan American Freeway NE, Albuquerque, NM 87113; telephone (505) 821-0055; web site: www.gruetwinery.com; e-mail: info@gruetwinery.com. Contact: Nathalie Gruet.

Heart of the Desert Vineyards: 7288 Highway 54/70, Alamogordo, NM 88310; telephone (505) 434-0035; web site: www.eagleranchpistachios. com; e-mail: eagleranch@zianet.com. Contact: Steve Jaszai.

Jacona Valley Vineyard: 311 County Road 84, Santa Fe, NM 87506; telephone (505) 660-7241; e-mail: jaconavalleyvineyard@msn.com. Contact: Trey Naylor.

La Chiripada Winery: Highway 75, Dixon, NM; telephone (505) 579-4437; web site: www.lachiripada.com; e-mail: chiripa@lachiripada. com. Contact: Minna Santos.

Las Parras de Abiquiu Vineyard Bed and Breakfast: 21341 Highway 84, Abiquiu, NM 87510; telephone (800) 817-5955; web site: www.lasparras. com; e-mail: lasparras@windstream.net. Contact: Arin or Stan Bader.

La Viña Winery: 4201 S. Highway 28, La Union, NM 88021; telephone (505) 882-7632; web site: www.lavinawinery.com; e-mail: stark@ lavinawinery.com. Contact: Denise or Ken Stark.

Los Luceros Winery: 183 County Road 41, Los Luceros, NM 87511; telephone (505) 747-3338; e-mail: los_luceros@cybermesa.com. Contact: Bruce Noel.

Luna Rossa Winery: 3710 W. Pine St., Deming, NM 88030; telephone (505) 544-1160; web site: www.lunarossawinery.com.

Madison Vineyards and Winery: HC 72, Box 490, Ribera, NM 87560; telephone (505) 421-8028; web site: www.madison-winery.com; e-mail: Madison@plateautel.net. Contact: Bill Madison.

Matheson Wine Company: 125 High Ridge Trail, Rio Rancho, NM 87124; telephone (505) 350-6557; web site: www.mathesonwines.com; e-mail: MDMatheson@yahoo.com. Contact: Mark Matheson.

Milagro Vineyards and Winery: 985 West Ella, Corrales, NM 87048; telephone (505) 898-3998; web site: www.milagrovineyardsandwinery.com; e-mail: wine@milagrowine.com. Contact: Mitzi or Rick Hobson.

Pecos Flavors Winery: 305 North Main St., Roswell, NM 88201; telephone (505) 627-6265; e-mail: pfwinery@qwest.net.

Ponderosa Valley Winery: 3171 Highway 290, Ponderosa, NM 87044; telephone (505) 834-7487; web site: www.ponderosawinery.com; e-mail: winemaker @ponderosawinery.com. Contact: Henry or Mary Street.

Ritchie-Slater Winery: County Road B-3, Number 10, Angel Fire, NM 87710; telephone (505) 377-6658; web site: www.ritchie-slaterwinery.com; e-mail: lanslater@hughes.net. Contact: Lan or Charlotte Slater.

Santa Fe Vineyards: 18348 Highway 84/285, Española, NM 87532; telephone (505) 753-8100; web site: www.santafevineyards.com; e-mail: dougharty@cybermesa.com. Contact: Dan Dougharty.

Sisneros-Torres Winery: 23 Winery Road North, Bosque, NM 87006; telephone (505) 249-9463; web site: www.sisnerosvineyards.com; e-mail: sisnerosray@aol.com.

Southwest Wines: 1325 DeBaca Road SE, Deming, NM 88030; telephone (505) 546-9324; web site: www.southwestwines.com; e-mail: flescombes@southwestwines.com. Contact: Florent Lescombes.

Tierra Encantada Winery: 1872 Five Points Road SW, Albuquerque, NM 87105; telephone (505) 764-9463; web site: www.tierra-encantada.com; e-mail: pat.coil@tierra-encantada.com. Contact: Pat Coil.

Tularosa Vineyards: 23 Coyote Canyon Road, Tularosa, NM 88352; telephone (505) 585-2260; web site: www.tularosavineyards.com; e-mail: wine@nmex.com. Contact: David Wickham.

Vivac Winery: 2075 Highway 68, Embudo, NM 87527; telephone (505) 579-4441; web site: www.vivacwinery.com; e-mail: info@vivacwinery.com. Contact: Chris Padberg.

Willmon Vineyards: 2801 Sudderth Drive, Ruidoso, NM 88345; telephone (505) 630-9463; web site: www.WinesOfNewMexico.com; e-mail: jessica@winesofnewmexico.com.

Wines of the San Juan Vineyard and Winery: 233 Highway 511, Blanco, NM 87412; telephone (505) 632-0879; web site: www.winesofthesanjuan.com; e-mail: winessanjuan@netscape.net. Contact David or Marcia Arnold.

Arizona

Alcantara Winery: 7500 E. Alcantara Way, Verde Valley, AZ 86326; telephone (928) 649-8463; web site: www.alcantaravineyard.com.

Arizona Vineyards: 1830 Patagonia Highway, Nogales, AZ 85621; telephone (520) 287-7972.

Broken Glass Vineyard and Winery Estates: Willcox, AZ.

Callaghan Vineyards: 336 Elgin Road, Elgin, AZ 85611; telephone (520) 455-5322; web site: www.callaghanvineyards.com; e-mail: Callaghan@dakota.net. Contact: Kent Callaghan.

Canelo Hills Vineyard and Winery: 342 Elgin Road, Elgin, AZ 85611; telephone (520) 455-5499; web site: www.canelohillswinery.com; e-mail: info@canelohillswinery.com. Contact: Tim or Joan Mueller.

Charron Vineyards: 18585 South Sonoita Highway, Vail, AZ 85641; telephone (520) 762-8585; web site: www.charronvineyards.com.

Cochise Groves/Golden Rule Vineyards: Cochise County, AZ.

Colibri Vineyards: 2825 Hilltop Road, Portal, AZ 85632; telephone (520) 558-2401; web site: www.colibrivineyard.com; e-mail: azvino@cox.net. Contact: Bob Johnson.

Coronado Vineyards: 2909 E. Country Club Dr., Willcox, AZ 85643; telephone (520) 384-2993; web site: www.coronadovineyards.com; e-mail: info@coronadovineyards.com. Contact: Jacque Cook.

Crop Circle Vineyards: 3052 N. Fort Grant Road, Willcox, AZ 85643; telephone (520) 384-3022; web site: www.echocanyonwinery.com; e-mail: sandcastles1111@aol.com. Contact: Gail or David Sparrow.

Dos Cabezas Wineworks: 3248 Highway 82, Sonoita, AZ 85637; telephone (520) 455-5141; web site: doscabezaswinery.com.

Echo Canyon Winery: Sedona, AZ; telephone (928) 634-8122; web site: www.echocanyonwinery.com.

Erath Vineyards: Willcox, AZ.

Fort Bowie Vineyards: 156 N. Jefferson St., Bowie, AZ 85605; telephone (520) 847-2593; web site: www.fortbowievineyards.net; e-mail: nuts4u@vtc.net. Contact: Torey Cranford.

Four Monkey Winery: Elgin, AZ; telephone (520) 455-9309.

Freitas Vineyard: Cottonwood, AZ; telephone (928) 639-2149.

Granite Creek Vineyards: 2515 N. Road 1 East, Chino Valley, AZ 86323; telephone (928) 636-2003; web site: www.granitecreekvineyards.com; e-mail: gcvineyards@cableone.net. Contact: Kit or Robin Hoult.

Hannah's Hill Vineyards: Sonoita, AZ.

Javelina Leap Winery: 1565 Page Springs Road, Cornville, AZ 86325; telephone (928) 274-0394; web site: www.javelinaleapwinery.com; e-mail: winemaker@commspeed.net. Contact: Rod Snapp.

Jerome Winery: 403 Clark St., Jerome, AZ 86331; telephone (928) 639-9067; web site: www.jeromewinery.com.

Keeling-Schaefer Vineyards: 10277 E. Rock Creek Ln., Pearce, AZ 85625; telephone (520) 824-2500; web site: www.keelingschaefervineyards.com; e-mail: Rod@keelingschaefervineyards.com. Contact: Rod Keeling.

Kief-Joshua Vineyards: 370 Elgin Road, Elgin, AZ 85611; telephone (520) 455-5582; web site: www.kiefjoshuavineyards.com; e-mail: kjvineyards@gmail.com. Contact: Kief Manning.

Kokopelli Winery: 35 W. Boston St., Chandler, AZ 85225; telephone (480) 792-6927; web site: www.kokopelliwinery.com; e-mail: Dennis@kokopelliwinery.com. Contact: Dennis Minchella.

Lightning Ridge Cellars: Sonoita, AZ.

Oak Creek Vineyards: 1555 Page Springs Road, Cornville, AZ 86325; telephone (928) 649-0290; web site: www.oakcreekvineyards.net.

Page Springs Cellars: 1500 N. Page Springs Rd., Cornville, AZ 86325; telephone (928) 639-3004; web site: www.pagespringscellars.com; e-mail: eric@pagespringscellars.com. Contact: Eric Glomski.

Painted Lady Vineyard: Skull Valley, AZ; telephone (928) 778-0933

Pillsbury Wine Company: Willcox, AZ; telephone (310) 508-3348; web site: www.pillsburywinecompany.com.

Rancho Rossa Vineyards: 32 Cattle Ranch Lane, Elgin, AZ 85611; telephone (520) 455-0700; web site: www.ranchorossa.com.

San Dominique: I-17 and Highway 169, Camp Verde, AZ 86322; telephone (602) 549-9787; web site: www.garlicparadise.com.

San Pedro Valley Vineyard: Benson, AZ.

Sonoita Crest: Sonoita, AZ.

Sonoita Vineyards: 290 Elgin-Canelo Road, Elgin, AZ 85611; telephone (520) 455-5893; web site: www.sonoitavineyards.com; e-mail: sonoitavineyards@peoplepc.com. Contact: Fran Lightly.

Su Vino Winery: 7035 E. Main St., Suite 110, Scottsdale, AZ 85251; telephone (480) 994-8466; web site: www.suvinowineryaz.com.

Sweet Sunrise Vineyard: Willcox, AZ 85643; telephone (520) 384-3787; web site: www.sweetsunrisevineyard.com.

Sycamore Canyon Winery: Page Springs, AZ; telephone (877) 903-9463.

Venado Cola Blanca Vineyard: Patagonia, AZ.

Village of Elgin Winery: The Elgin Complex, Elgin, AZ 85611; telephone (520) 455-9309; web site: www.elginwines.com; e-mail: info@elginwines.com.

Wilhelm Family Vineyard: Elgin, AZ; telephone (520)455-9291.

UTAH

Castle Creek Winery: Highway 128, Mile 14, Moab, UT 84532; telephone (435) 259-3332; web site: www.castlecreekwinery.com; e-mail: charleen @castlecreekwinery.com. Contact: Charleen Radley.

La Caille Winery: 9565 Wasatch Blvd., Little Cottonwood Canyon, UT 84092; telephone (801) 942-1751; web site: www.lacaille.com; e-mail: laura @lacaille.com. Contact: Laura Horton.

Native Wines: 72 S. 500 W. 63, Mt. Pleasant, UT 84647; telephone (435) 462-9261; web site: www.nativewines.net.

Round Mountain Vineyards: 230 Miller Lane, Castle Valley, UT 84532; telephone (435) 259-1927; web site: www.RoundMountainVineyardsand Winery.com; e-mail: janderson53@sisna.com.

Spanish Valley Vineyards and Winery: 4710 S. Zimmerman Lane, Moab, UT 84532; telephone (435) 259-8134; web site: www.Moab-Utah.com/ SpanishValleyWinery; e-mail: spanishvalleyvineyards@yahoo.com. Contact: Stacy Dezelsky.

Summum Winery: 707 Genessee Ave., Salt Lake City, UT 84104; telephone (801) 355-0137.

William Cooper Winery: 976 S. 800 E, Salt Lake City, UT 84105; telephone (801) 575-2110.

COLORADO

Alfred Eames Cellars at Puesta del Sol Vineyards: 11931 4050 Road, Paonia, CO 81428; telephone (970) 527-3269; web site: www.alfredeamescellars.com; e-mail: eames@alfredeamescellars.com.

Amber Ridge Vineyards: 3820 G .25 Road, Palisade, CO 81526; telephone (970) 464-5314; web site: www.amberridgevineyards.com; e-mail: corvinyrd@aol.com.

Augustina's Winery: 4715 N. Broadway B-3, Boulder, CO 80304; telephone (303) 545-2047; web site: www.winechick.biz; e-mail: winechic@boulder.net. Contact: Marianne Walter.

Avanti Winery: 9046 W. Bowles Ave., Littleton, CO 80123; telephone (303) 904-7650; web site: www.avantiwinery.com; e-mail: grifgarman@aol.com.

Balistreri Vineyards: 1946 E. 66th Ave., Denver, CO 80229; telephone (303) 287-5156; web site: www.balistreriwine.com; e-mail: info@balistreriwine.com. Contact: Julie Balistreri.

Barton Creek Cellars: 240 Lake Dillon Drive, Dillon, CO 80435; telephone (303) 956-9267; web site: www.breckenridgewinery.com; e-mail: info@breckenridgewinery.com.

Black Bridge Winery: 15836 Black Bridge Road, Paonia, CO 81428; telephone (970) 527-6838; web site: www.coloradowineonline.com.

Black Canyon Vineyards: 29987 Stinaley Gulch Rd., Hotchkiss, CO 81419; telephone (970) 872-4250; web site: www.blackcanyonwine.com; e-mail: kchilds@kcfpc.com. Contact: Kim Childs.

Blossomwood Cidery: 794 NE Indian Camp Ave., Cedaredge, CO 81413; telephone (970) 856-3220; web site: www.blossomwoodcidery.com; e-mail: info@blossomwoodcidery.com. Contact: Janese Carney.

Bonacquisti Wine Company: 4640 Pecos St., Unit I, Denver, CO 80211; telephone (303) 477-9463; web site: www.DenverWine.net; e-mail: paul@denverwine.net.

Bookcliff Vineyards: 1501 Lee Hill Rd. No. 17, Boulder, CO 80304; telephone (303) 499-7301; web site: www.bookcliffvineyards.com; e-mail: john@bookcliffvineyards.com; Contact John Garlich.

Boulder Creek Winery: 6440 Odell Place, Boulder, CO 80304; telephone (303) 516-9031; e-mail: bouldercreekwine@msn.com. Contact: Jackie Thompson.

Canyon Wind Cellars: 3907 North River Rd., Palisade, CO 81526; telephone (970) 464-0888; web site: www.canyonwindcellars.com; e-mail: j.e. Christianson@gmail.com. Contact: Jay Christianson.

Carlson Vineyards: 461 35 Road, Palisade, CO 81526; telephone (970) 464-5554; web site: www.carlsonvineyards.com; e-mail: cobw13@acsol.net.

Ciatano Winery: 16858 N. St. Vrain Dr., Lyons, CO 80540; telephone (303) 823-5011; web site: www.ciatanowinery.com. Contact Mary Lou Gibson.

Colorado Cellars Winery: 3553 E Road, Palisade, CO 81526; telephone (800) 848-2812; web site: www.coloradocellars.com; e-mail: info@coloradocellars.com. Contact: Richard or Padte Turley.

Colorado Wine Room and Talon Winery: 455 Kokopelli Blvd., Unit A, Fruita, CO 81521; telephone (970) 858-6330; web site: www.coloradowineroom.com.

Concetta Cellars: 4637 North Foxtail Dr., Castle Rock, CO 80109; telephone (303) 663-0110; web site: www.concettacellars.com; e-mail: info@concettacellars.com.

Confre Cellars: 785 Elberta Ave., Palisade, CO 81526; telephone (970) 464-1300; e-mail: stkathryn@yahoo.com.

Cottonwood Cellars: 5482 Highway 348, Olathe, CO 81425; telephone (970) 323-6224; web site: www.cottonwoodcellars.com; e-mail: cottonwoodwines@cs.com. Contact: Diana Read.

Creekside Cellars: 28036 Highway 74, Evergreen, CO 80439; telephone (303) 674-5460; web site: www.creeksidecellars.net; e-mail: creeksidewines@aol.com.

DeBeque Canyon Winery: 3943 Highway 6, Palisade, CO 81526; telephone (970) 464-0550; web site: www.debequecanyonwinery.com; e-mail: debequecanyonwines@bresnan.net.

Desert Moon Vineyards: 3349.5 C Road, Palisade, CO 81526; telephone (303) 884-5044; web site: www.desertmoonvineyards.com; e-mail: debra_ray@desertmoonvineyards.com.

D'VineWine: 358 Blue River Parkway, Unit G, Silverthorne, CO 80498; telephone (970) 485-3742; web site: www.winerysilverthorne.com.

Garfield Estates Winery: 3572 G Road, Palisade, CO 81526; telephone (970) 464-0941; web site: www.garfieldestates.com; e-mail: info@garfieldestates.com. Contact: Brad Harmon.

Grande River Vineyards: 787 N. Elberta Ave., Palisade, CO 81526; telephone (970) 464-5867; web site: www.granderiverwines.com; e-mail: info@granderiverwines.com.

Graystone Winery: 3352 F Road, Clifton, CO 81520; telephone (970) 434-8610; web site: www.graystonewine.com; e-mail: graystonewinery@aol.com.

Guy Drew Vineyards: 20057 Road G, Cortez, CO 81321; telephone (970) 565-4958; web site: www.guydrewvineyards.com; e-mail: guydrew@fone.net. Contact: Guy or Ruth Drew.

Hermosa Vineyards: 3269 ¾ C Road, Palisade, CO 81526; telephone (970) 434-8766; web site: www.hermosavineyards.com; e-mail: hermosavineyards@aol.com.

Iron Mountain Winery: 1 West Flatiron Circle, Suite 336, Broomfield, CO 80021; telephone (303) 464-9463; web site: www.ironmountainwinery.com; e-mail: info@inronmountainwinery.com.

Jack Rabbit Hill Winery: 26567 North Road, Hotchkiss, CO 81419; telephone (970) 835-3677; web site: www.jackrabbithill.com; e-mail: lance@jackrabbithill.com. Contact: Lance or Anna Hanson.

J. Susi Winery: 26832 Barkley Road, Conifer, CO 80433; telephone (303) 717-1527; web site: www.jsusiwinery.com; e-mail: johnpsusi@hotmail.com.

Leroux Creek Vineyards: 12388-3100 Road, Hotchkiss, CO 81419; telephone (970) 872-4746; web site: www.lerouxcreekinn.com; e-mail: info@lerouxcreek.com. Contact: Joanna Gilbert or Yvon Gros.

Meadery of the Rockies: 3701 G Road, Palisade, CO 81526; telephone (970) 464-7899; web site: www.meadery-of-the-rockies.com; e-mail: stkathryn@yahoo.com.

Medovina Winery: Niwot, CO 80544; telephone (303) 845-3090; web site: www.medovina.com; e-mail: mark@medovina.com.

Mesa Park Vineyards: 3321 C Road, Palisade, CO 81526; telephone (970) 434-4191.

Minturn Cellars: 107 Williams St., Minturn, CO 81645; telephone (970) 827-4065; web site: www.minturncellars.com.

Mountain Spirit Winery: 16150 County Road 220, Salida, CO 81201; telephone (719) 539-1175; web site: www.mountainspiritwinery.com; e-mail: barkett@mountainspiritwinery.com. Contact: Terry or Michael Barkett.

Mountain View Winery and Orchard: 5859 58.25 Road, Olathe, CO 81425; telephone (970) 323-6816; web site: www.mountainviewwinery.com; e-mail: mgyoung4@yahoo.com. Contact: Wendy or Mike Young.

Pikes Peak Vineyards and Winery: 3901 Janitell Road, Colorado Springs, CO 80906; telephone (719) 576-0075.

Plum Creek Cellars: 3708 G Road, Palisade, CO 81526; telephone (970) 464-7586; web site: www.plumcreekwinery.com; e-mail: info@plumcreekwinery.com.

Redstone Meadery: 4700 Pearl St., No. 2A, Boulder, CO 80301; telephone (720) 406-1215; web site: www.redstonemeadery.com; e-mail: david@redstonemeadery.com. Contact: David Myers.

Reeder Mesa Vineyards: 7799 Reeder Mesa Rd., Whitewater, CO 81527; telephone (970) 242-7468; web site: www.ReederMesaWines.com; e-mail: reedermesawines@hughes.net. Contact: Doug or Kris Vogel.

Snowy Peaks Winery: 292 Moraine Ave., Estes Park, CO 80517; telephone (970) 586-2099; web site: www.snowypeakswinery.com; e-mail: info@snowypeakswinery.com.

Spero Winery: 3316 W. 64th Ave., Denver, CO 80221; telephone (720) 519-1506; e-mail: sperowinery@aol.com.

Spruce Mountain Meadery: 1218 Yarnell Dr., Larkspur, CO 80118; telephone (719) 351-4910; web site: www.sprucemountainmeadery.com; e-mail: info@sprucemountainmeadery.com. Contact: Gretchen Bliss.

S. Rhodes Vineyards: 13450 Chickory Road, Hotchkiss, CO 81419; telephone (970) 872-4925.

St. Kathryn Cellars Winery: 785 Elberta Ave., Palisade, CO 81526; telephone (970) 464-9288; web site: www.st-kathryn-cellars.com; e-mail: stkathryn@yahoo.com.

Stone Cottage Cellars: 41716 Reds Road, Paonia, CO 81428; telephone (970) 527-3444; web site: www.stonecottagecellars.com; e-mail: info@stonecottagecellars.com. Contact: Karen Helleckson.

Stoney Mesa Winery and Ptarmigan Vineyards: 221 31 3/10 Road, Grand Junction, CO 81503; telephone (970) 434-2015; web site: www.stoneymesa.com; e-mail: ronneal@stoneymesa.com. Contact: Ron Neal.

Surface Creek Winery: 12983 Highway 65, Eckert, CO 81418; telephone (970) 835-9463; web site: www.surfacecreek.com; e-mail: winery@ surfacecreek.com.

Sutcliffe Vineyards: 12202 Road G, Cortez, CO 81321; telephone (970) 565-0825; web site: www.sutcliffewines.com; e-mail: battlerock@frontier.net.

Terror Creek Winery: 17445 Garvin Mesa Road, Paonia, CO 81428; telephone (970) 527-3484; e-mail: jmath@paonia.com. Contact: Joan Mathewson.

The Winery at Holy Cross Abbey: 3011 E. Highway 50, Cañon City, CO 81212; telephone (719) 276-2297; web site: www.abbeywinery.com; e-mail: info@abbbeywinery.com. Contact: Sally Cookson.

Trail Ridge Winery: 4113 W. Eisenhower Blvd., Loveland, CO 80537; telephone (970) 635-0949; web site: www.trwinery.com. Contact: Tim Merrick.

Turquoise Mesa Winery: 555 Burbank St., Q, Broomfield, CO 80020; telephone (303) 653-3822; web site: www.turquoisemesawinery.com; e-mail: tabwine@aol.com. Contact: Mary Joan Bueb.

Two Rivers Winery and Chateau: 2087 Broadway, Grand Junction, CO 81503; telephone (970)255-1471; web site: www.tworiverswinery.com; e-mail: billie@tworiverswinery.com. Contact: Billie Witham.

Varaision Vineyards and Winery: 405 W. 1st St., Palisade, CO 81526; telephone (970) 464-4928; web site: www.varaisionvineyards.com; e-mail: conifer@quixnet.net.

Verso Cellars: Cooper Creek Square, Suite 231, Winter Park, CO 80482; telephone (970) 726-9430; web site: www.versocellars.com; e-mail: wine@versocellars.com.

Whitewater Hill Vineyards: 220 32 Road, Grand Junction, CO 81503; telephone (970) 434-6868; web site: www.whitewaterhill.com; e-mail: info@whitewaterhill.com. Contact: Nancy Janes.

Winter Park Winery: 395 Zerex St., Fraser, CO 80442; telephone (970) 726-4514; web site: www.winterparkwinery.com; e-mail: jon@winterparkwinery.com.

Woody Creek Cellars: Woody Creek, CO 81656; telephone (970) 923-2253; web site: www.woodycreekcellars.com

Selected Bibliography

Arizona Wine Growers Association

Fay, A. 2002, *The Story of Colorado Wines*, Western Reflections
Publishing Company, Montrose, Colorado. ISBN 1-890437-73-5.

MacNeil, K. 2001, *The Wine Bible*, Workman Publishing Company, New
York. ISBN-10: 1-56305-434-5.

New Mexico Winegrowers Association

Rocky Mountain Association of Vintners and Viticulturists

Sandersier, A., 2005, *The Wines of New Mexico*, University of New Mexico
Press, Albuquerque. ISBN 0-8263-3252-8.

Smith, Alta & Brad, 2002, *The Guide to Colorado Wineries*, Fulcrum
Publishing, Golden. ISBN 1-55591-314-8.

Street, H.K., 1997, *The History of Wine in New Mexico, 400 Years of
Struggle*, Ponderosa Valley Vineyards and Winery, Ponderosa,
New Mexico.

Acknowledgements

My interest in vineyards and wineries began in 2006 when my husband, Beauford Thompson, and I planted a small vineyard, following in the footsteps of other new vintners in southeastern Wyoming. I discovered that most people did not know that wine grapes could be grown in the harsh climate of the high plains states. My first book about the vineyards and wineries of South Dakota, Wyoming and Nebraska inspired me to seek out additional entrepreneurs who were planting grapes and making wine in new areas of the country.

We subsequently traveled many roads leading to the vintners of the four corners states of New Mexico, Arizona, Utah and Colorado. I was once again awed by the stories of these new-age pioneers. My appreciation goes to all of the people who answered my initial mailed questionnaire, and to those folks who were gracious in giving their time and knowledge for a personal interview.

A very special thank you goes to Marge Black Graziano for providing us lodging in her cottage in Jerome, Arizona, while we conducted the Arizona interviews. My friend, Karen Halderson, also provided housing for part of our journey in New Mexico. Everyone welcomed us with enthusiasm and often provided food and drink.

I thank my husband, Beauford Thompson, for his patience on each journey, for chauffeuring duties, and for encouragement.

My appreciation goes to Olga Crespin for manuscript editing and to Dan Hashberger for editing and design.

My deepest gratitude goes to my readers and to the members of our fledgling grape growers group in Chugwater, Wyoming.

ABOUT THE AUTHOR

Starley Talbott was raised on and currently resides on a Wyoming ranch. She is a graduate of the University of Wyoming and the University of Nevada, Reno. She has been a freelance writer for more than 30 years and is a former Wyoming newspaper reporter and photographer.

After living most of her life in Wyoming, Starley continued her journey through life while living in several states and foreign countries. At the age of 60 she joined the Peace Corps and served briefly in South Africa. She has taught conversational English in Peru and China. Starley detailed her world travels in her first book, *Lasso the World, A western writer's tales of folks around the globe,* telling the stories of people in many countries including the United States.

In 2006 Starley married her old high school sweetheart, Beauford Thompson, and they began a new journey by planting a small vineyard in southeastern Wyoming. This brought the opportunity to write about the vineyards and wineries of South Dakota, Wyoming and Nebraska in Starley's second book, *Along the Grapevine Trail,* published in 2008 by the South Dakota State Historical Society Press.

Four Corners: The Vineyards and Wineries of New Mexico, Arizona, Utah and Colorado is Starley's third book. It will soon be followed by a pictorial history of *Platte County, Wyoming,* to be published by Arcadia Publishing Company.

Starley and Beauford divide their time between their vineyard in Wyoming, a home in Colorado, and travel.